STRANGE
BEASTS
OF CHINA

TRANSLATED BY

STRANGE BEASTS OF CHINA

YAN GE

JEREMY TIANG

TILTED AXIS PRESS

兽 [shòu] – beast

Originally used to describe the act of hunting, the meaning of the word shifted over time to the object of the hunt, the prey. More than a neutral word for animal, 兽 denotes the absence of humanity, and carries the connotations of savagery and wildness.

SORROWFUL BEASTS

As the Splendid River flows through Yong'an City's centre and heads east, it separates into the Lotus and Peacock Rivers in Luoding District. The sorrowful beasts live in a housing development on the Peacock's southern bank, in the north-eastern quarter of the city.

These old buildings, their walls thick with ivy, are known as the Leye Estate. They were originally built as dormitories for the Ping Le Cotton Mill, where many of the sorrowful beasts have worked for years, ever since they first came to Yong'an City from the south and settled here.

Sorrowful beasts are gentle by nature, and prefer the cold and dark. They love cauliflower and mung beans, vanilla ice cream and tangerine pudding. They fear trains, bitter gourd and satellite TV.

The males of the species are tall, with large mouths and small hands, scales on the insides of their left calves and fins attached to their right ears. The skin around their belly buttons is dark green. Other than that, they're just like regular people.

The females are beautiful – slender figures with reddish skin, long, narrow eyes, ears a little larger than normal. For three days at the full moon, they lose the ability of human speech and squawk like birds instead. Otherwise, they're just like regular people.

Sorrowful beasts never smile. If they do, they can't stop – not until they die. Hence their name.

If you look back far enough, you might trace their forebears to a poet from ancient times, too far back for there to be any evidence.

Male sorrowful beasts are skilled with their hands, which is how they ended up weaving textiles. The females, being good-looking, often work as salesgirls in the fabric stores. The people of Yong'an City come shopping for textiles to this dilapidated little district all the way across town, just so they can catch a glimpse of these attractive beasts.

Legend has it that a sorrowful beast's smile is so beautiful, no one who sees it could ever forget it. But no matter how many jokes you tell them, they never laugh, let alone smile.

This makes the loveliness of the female beasts all the more to be prized and pitied, and the tycoons of Yong'an City take pride in marrying them – the females can mate with people and produce human offspring. The males can't do this, and so Leye Estate is filled with desolate bachelors, while the ladies end up in the wealthy district to the south, having fled so fast their feet barely touched the ground, their faces like ice.

At one point, the city's zoologists raised an outcry in the newspapers: if things went on like this, these rare creatures would surely go extinct. And so the government passed a law: sorrowful beasts could only marry their own kind. If they wished to couple with a human, special permission would be required, and could only be balloted for once every five years. As a result, having a beast-wife became an even greater status symbol, and the extra demand from the elite greatly increased the government's revenue.

—

Lefty, an artist, was the friend of a friend. The stories about her and the sorrowful beast had spread far and wide among our circle, but few people knew the truth of the matter. One day, she came up to me at a party and said, 'I know you specialise in beastly tales. I want to tell you a sorrowful beast's story. Are you interested?'

'Yes,' I said, 'but I have to pay you something.'

'I don't want anything.'

'That's the rule,' I said, 'I have to give you some-thing.' I smiled, but her face remained blank.

She said, 'I'd love a vanilla ice cream.'

I bought her one, and she devoured it with gusto.

I'd smoked two cigarettes before she finally spoke.

She said, 'My sorrowful beast died last week.'

———

Lefty met the male beast at a time when the Ping Le Mill was doing badly – all the salesgirls had run off to marry tycoons, leaving no one to sell the goods. Many mill workers had been laid off. She first encountered him at the Dolphin Bar – he'd walked over and said to her, 'I've just lost my job, could you buy me a drink?'

She looked up at him. He was very tall, with a serious expression, the skin of his face shiny and unwrinkled. 'All right,' she said. As they drank, Lefty noticed an exquisite fin behind his ear. She said, 'You're a beast.' He answered, 'Yes, and I'm out of work.'

That night, he followed her home, and she tamed him. His name was Cloud. He slept quietly at night, didn't talk much, loved baths, and ate nothing but three vanilla ice creams a day. If anyone turned on the

TV, he'd let out a shattering howl and his eyes would flash red – his beastly nature revealing itself.

Lefty stopped watching television. When she got home, they'd sit at either end of the sofa, each reading a book. When he was happy, he'd let out a long cat-like rumble, but he never smiled.

At night they slept together, Cloud in the nude. His physique was just like a human male's. The skin around his belly button was green as the sea, even a little translucent. Lefty often found herself mesmerised by that patch of skin. 'It's so beautiful,' she'd say.

She stroked him, and he purred like a contented cat, but they couldn't make love. 'It's because you're human,' he explained.

They slept in each other's arms, like a couple of beasts.

It was a lovely time. The male beast was even more nurturing and resourceful than a human girl – he cooked for Lefty and washed her clothes. The food was mostly vegetarian, and the laundry had a strange fragrance. As Lefty ate, he'd watch from across the table, his expression tender. She thought of him almost as her husband.

This all happened last May. Lefty painted quite a few portraits of Cloud, and held a very successful exhibition at Evergreen Gallery. Everyone knew she had a sorrowful beast as her model, with long, sturdy legs, a flat, greenish stomach, and bright, empty eyes. Standing or sitting, he became an object of affection for all the young women in the city.

—

I saw that exhibition. The first rumours I heard about Lefty and the sorrowful beast were from our gossip king, Charley. 'That Lefty girl definitely slept with him,' he said.

I said, 'Male beasts can't do it with humans.'

Charley sniggered. 'You believe that?'

Yet I did believe he was a pure beast. In one of Lefty's paintings, he sat on a windowsill, not a stitch on him, clearly exposing the scales on his calf. His expression was a little shy, and therefore captivating. Everyone thought how beautiful he'd be, if he would only smile.

But he didn't.

If he smiled, he would die.

'He's dead,' said Lefty now. She sat across from me, taking great mouthfuls of her ice cream. She looked terrible, not smiling either.

—

Lefty said that on the night of a full moon, they had

heard a long cry, like a phoenix. Cloud's eyes had widened. In a panic, he ran to open the door. A girl was standing outside. Even in the murky light of the corridor, you could see she was gorgeous. She couldn't speak, she just let out another cry, then hugged him tightly.

Lefty asked her to come in and gave her a vanilla ice cream. The girl's skin was flushed, as if blood was about to seep from it. Cloud said, 'She's sick.'

This female beast was his sister, Rain, who was married to a rich man from the southern district. Now she clung to Cloud as they walked to the living room. They got her to drink a tincture of woad leaf, and still she wouldn't stop shrilling. Cloud didn't know what to do, so he called the human husband, only to have him snap in frustration, 'She keeps screeching, and I don't know what she wants – after all, I'm not a beast!'

Cloud hung up and hugged his sister, kissing her cheeks over and over again. Both beasts were now letting out similar cries. Sitting in the armchair across from them, Lefty phoned her ex-boyfriend, Dr Fu.

The doctor hurried over, looking – according to Lefty – more handsome than ever before. He nimbly took Rain's temperature and blood pressure, then said she was pregnant, and gave her an injection.

Lefty called Rain's husband, who was so over-joyed he could barely speak. Practically in tears, he choked, 'Thank the heavens, an heir for the Wang family!' Lefty hung up in a rage. Next thing she knew, a Mercedes-Benz was pulling up outside. When they said goodbye to Rain, she was still shrieking non-stop, though her skin was regaining its colour now.

Cloud was all sweaty, and went to take a shower. Dr Fu paced around the living room, then suddenly embraced Lefty and said, 'I've missed you.'

They stayed with their arms wrapped around each other, reminiscing about bygone days, touching and kissing, their breaths urgent. As they tangled, the splashes from the bathroom were like the warm embrace of ocean waves.

The next morning, Cloud was dead.

Lefty said, 'He never smiled. I don't know how he died.'

I said, 'I don't know either.'

The artist looked distraught, which made her even more beautiful. She said, 'I want to know how he died, I was practically in love with him.'

—

That night, the party ended abruptly. Outside the clubhouse, I saw Lefty and a man drive off in an expensive sports car, tyres squealing with glee.

The man next to me couldn't stop praising her. 'Ever since she got herself a sorrowful beast, she's a new woman. Her paintings are more stunning than ever, and so is she – wonder when I'll find one for myself.'

He turned to me. 'Aren't you supposed to know about these things? Go find me one.'

'It takes destiny for a human to tame a beast,' I said.

He wasn't having it. 'How many beasts are there in Yong'an City? In the end, who knows who's taming whom.'

I laughed. 'If you're scared, you should leave.'

'No one who comes here is able to leave,' he said. 'This city is too full of monsters, too enchanting, too bewitching. A paradise for artists and wanderers.'

I thought of Lefty as I walked home. I'd heard that when she first arrived here from the north, she was as coarse as gravel and had a strong country accent. People laughed at her behind her back. And now, many years later, she'd become an elegant lady with lips the colour of blood, as if she'd been in the city all her life.

—

The sorrowful beasts came to the city many years ago

and never left, never mind the dire warnings of zoologists, never mind floods or droughts or recessions or wars or stock market crashes or epidemics. They just stayed put in Yong'an, their numbers stable, like an eternal riddle.

Fifty or sixty years ago, Yong'an had a great many beasts, and human beings were just one breed among them; but then war broke out, and amid this unrest, people battled the beasts for an entire decade. This period of history vanished from the annals. It wasn't all that long ago, but everyone knows, or pretends to know, only the barest facts about it. Most of the beasts vanished, driven to extinction. The sorrowful beasts survived, and became the most populous tribe in Yong'an City.

But no human could truly understand the mysteries of these creatures' existences. The females married out, but the males couldn't mate with people.

I went online to search for information about sorrowful beasts, trying to find out how Cloud might have died, but I found no leads apart from these scraps.

'Maybe he ate too much bitter gourd and it killed him,' I joked.

I called my university professor, a renowned Yong'an zoologist. 'Have you researched sorrowful beasts? I need to know what could suddenly kill them, apart from smiling.'

He was silent for a moment. 'Meet me for coffee tomorrow, we'll talk then.'

—

In the morning paper, I read a story about Lefty in the entertainment section – she'd been spotted on numerous dates with the son of a well-known construction magnate. In the accompanying pictures, they were drinking at a rooftop bar, the man young and dashing, grinning smugly. You could make out Lefty's side profile, an eye-catching hoop dangling from one ear, her features exquisite. She was calm and melancholy, unsmiling.

I took a sip of tea, and then another, and wondered if she was still in love with the dead beast.

The phone rang just then – my professor again. 'Have you seen today's paper? The picture of the lady painter?'

'That's what I wanted to ask you about – it was her sorrowful beast who died.'

A long silence. 'Listen, it's best if you don't go poking into this.'

'Why?' I asked. 'Do you know how that beast died?'

'He may not have died.' Another pause. 'His soul

might be immortal.'

I laughed. 'You're talking about the City of the Dead?'

The City of the Dead was a place that, according to legend, lay beneath Yong'an City. Humans and beasts, cars and roads, rock bands and their followers, all living forever. Every mother scared her child with this horror story: 'Don't spend too long reading in the toilet, because while you're distracted, a soul might rise up through the pipes and possess your body.' This gave us all a healthy fear of lingering in the toilet, and it was only when we grew up that we realised we'd been tricked.

When I was still a little girl, I used to squat by the toilet for a long time, staring, hoping a soul would float up to talk with me. Human or beast would be fine. If one showed up, I'd say hello. That's the sort of courteous child I was. It was sure to like me.

The phone was buzzing, the signal weak. The professor said, 'Anyway... what I meant was—' We got cut off.

—

I visited the female beast Rain in the wealthy district to the south. She greeted me politely in the hall, her belly already faintly swelling. 'I've read your novels.

They're very good.'

She was drinking iced chocolate, and her skin glowed pearly pink, her voice soft and warm. She sat in a corner of the room, back to the light, eyes gleaming black.

A sense of unease prickled me. 'I'm here to ask about your brother.'

Rain's face was blank. 'Brother? I don't have a brother.'

As I gaped at her, the security guard briskly walked in from the outer chamber. 'Madam isn't feeling well, miss,' he said. 'You should come again another day.'

He was very tall and expressionless, the spitting image of a sorrowful beast, though he was human. With a big, strong hand, he led me by the arm. 'This way, miss.'

Rain remained on the sofa, watching me guilelessly. She said, 'What's wrong?' Her ears were a little larger than average, making her look like a temple Buddha floating among the clouds, unaware of worldly torments, asking his acolytes, 'If they're hungry, why not just have a meat bun?'

That night, at the Dolphin Bar, I ran into Charley with his new girlfriend, a timid-looking lady who sipped a glass of orange juice and sat silently next to us.

I bummed a cigarette off him, and told him what had happened that morning. 'It's infuriating,' I said, 'Getting pushed around like that.'

I blew smoke right at his face, and he frowned as he waved it away. He said, 'It's not like you're new to this, didn't you know this would happen? You can't blame anybody else.'

—

Our local government was on People's Road, a cluster of unappealing squat grey buildings, with guards standing ramrod straight by the front entrance. Too many to take in at a single glance. God knows how many documents were pumped out into the world each day to be circulated, proclaimed, or peeped at.

Among these were the regulations for marriages between sorrowful beasts and humans: beforehand, the female beast should undergo hypnosis or surgery to eliminate her beastly memory, and have monthly hormone shots to suppress her beastly nature. This meant all beasts with human husbands had amnesia. They didn't know who they were, or even that they were beasts. They sat in their sumptuous living rooms, waiting for their husbands to come home, then disrobed and got into bed with them, perpetuating the human race. Yet when the moon was full, they'd recover their beastliness, losing the power of speech. Afterwards, they forgot what had passed in those two or three days.

It seemed a new type of hormone was being invented that would leave the beasts unable to remember anything of their origins, even when the moon was at its roundest, ensuring they would remain human all their lives. They'd still be unable to smile, though, let alone laugh – if they did, they wouldn't be able to stop, and then they'd die.

I phoned my professor and asked if there was really any such thing. He flew into a temper and yelled, 'If there isn't, then who wrote that article for you? The one on this topic, just three months ago? I can't believe I taught a loser like you. Imagine ending up as a novelist!'

I quickly hung up, then picked up the receiver again, meaning to call Lefty, but I couldn't make myself do it.

Nights in Yong'an City were full of animal cries of no discernible origin. I was born here, and got used to it early on. My mother used to tell me, 'You can't be sure that beasts aren't people, or that people aren't just another type of beast.'

But that wasn't how things were. People would always be scared of beasts.

I put down the phone again. Someone was sobbing quietly, someone was hugging me tightly and weeping. Someone was saying, 'Hello, hello, hello.'

I lived alone on the seventeenth floor of Peach Blossom Villas, the Splendid River visible in the distance. My spacious flat was empty, but still I heard crying. 'Stop that,' I said.

But it continued.

—

The painter Lefty was behaving a little erratically. She kept calling to tell me stories about her and the beast. I understood she had no one to talk to, and asked, 'What do you want in return for these tales?'

She didn't want anything, she already had everything, and she'd never get anything again.

Now and then, I'd see her in the papers. A beautiful artist will always have someone to love her. A young, wealthy human male, his eyes full of exuberance. On the phone, she sobbed, 'I've been getting these headaches recently, I'm always so confused, I don't know who I am.'

She couldn't find her sorrowful beast, the one who belonged to her. She'd tamed him. He'd stayed with her, mostly silent, drawn to dark and damp places, fond of ice cream, sweet-natured, empty-eyed, preferring to go without clothes, to wander naked around the flat – and she'd painted every one of his movements, the mesmerising green patch on his belly that somehow seemed to be expanding.

She said his body was cool, which made it hard to keep your hands off him on summer nights. At times he'd let out a low moan, at times he spoke, but mostly he preferred the former. He was a beast. The scales on his leg gave off such a dazzling light.

Perhaps he really was the descendant of a poet, melancholy by nature.

I went back to the gallery where she'd held her exhibition, but all the portraits of Cloud had already been sold. I asked the owner who'd bought them. He stammered and refused to tell me, so I deployed Charley's name.

'It was Mr He,' said the owner. 'He Qi.'

He Qi. He Qi. I quickly found the face – I'd just seen him in the papers. He was Lefty's boyfriend, the prominent Yong'an construction magnate's son.

———

Mr He Qi turned out to be a reader of my books. I sat in his vast reception room, clutching a cup of Blue Mountain coffee, my attention somewhat unmoored. I asked, 'Did you buy all the paintings of that beast?'

'Yes,' he answered, nothing evasive about his beaming face.

'Why?'

'I'm in love,' he said, still smiling.

'In love?'

'Yes.'

I hesitated. 'Do you mean with the beast,' I said, 'or the painter?'

He smiled, not responding.

'He died, you know,' I said.

'Who?'

'The beast.'

'Did he die? He didn't die, his soul is immortal.'

'I mean...'

'Does it really matter? I'm looking forward to your next novel.'

—

The Ping Le Cotton Mill stood along the lower reaches of the Peacock River. It produced well-stitched blankets, bed sheets and towels to be shipped far and wide. Because the male beasts were so skilled with their hands, they held sway here, more or less dominating the market in Yong'an City. But their lives were hard, because the government imposed such high taxes on them. Charley whispered to me about what our leaders were saying behind the scenes. He claimed they were relying on the placid natures of the sorrowful beasts, otherwise there'd have been a revolt long ago!

At the entrance to Leye Estate was Yong'an's largest ice cream distribution centre. A gang of young male beasts hung around, staring at the attached shop. I asked one of them if I could buy him a cone. He nodded eagerly. Sitting across from me as he slurped his ice cream happily, he said, 'Auntie, you're a good person.'

'Why don't you call me Big Sister instead?'

He obligingly switched. 'Big Sister,' he murmured.

I asked how old he was. He said he was five.

We sat in a little park outside Leye Estate. The walls were covered in layers of ivy, making the buildings look like countless enormous trees, birds of paradise resting on their branches after long migrations.

'What are you looking at?' he asked.

'It's so pretty.'

The little beast seemed startled. 'What's that on your face?'

'A smile,' I said.

'Smile?'

'Yes.'

'Why can't I do that?'

'You can't smile,' I told him. 'You'd die if you did.'

'I see,' he said. 'How interesting.' He looked relaxed, while it was I who felt uneasy. 'You call that a smile, but we call it pain. My daddy says when the pain reaches its end, we die.'

'Would you like another ice cream?' I said, to change the subject.

'Yes, please.'

I bought him another one, which he attacked with delight, until a long cry came from the distance, like the roar of nature itself.

He said he had to go home. 'Bye-bye Big Sister. You're such a nice person, when I'm grown up I'll marry you.'

I smiled again. 'You're too young. Besides, you can't marry me, I'm human.'

'I can. My daddy says I can, but if I do, you'll laugh.'

'Laugh?'

He turned, his silhouette like a god in the gloom. 'That's right. You people would say, you'll die.'

———

The next time I saw our resident troublemaker Charley at the Dolphin Bar, he had a different girl-friend. I said, 'Did you know He Qi bought all of Lefty's sorrowful beast paintings?'

Charley looked sidelong at me. 'Of course I know. Why the big fuss? No wonder you've never amounted to anything.'

He went on, 'I was the one who brought the two together. He Qi saw those paintings and came pestering me for an introduction to Lefty. I gave him her phone number.'

'And then?'

'And then the same old story. He Qi called and said they'd finally met in person. He was enchanted by the beast.'

'The same beast?'

'Yes. He Qi said he loved him.'

That night, Lefty phoned me. She and He Qi were sparking like crazy and she'd forgotten all about the beast. I said, a little angrily, 'I thought you were so in love with Cloud.'

She was quiet, then asked, 'Is love possible between humans and beasts? Not the ones who marry rich men, the ones who have so much surgery and hormone shots, they believe they're people. The ones who're still beasts. Can they be in love with humans?

'I love He Qi,' the painter concluded.

—

As the legends tell us, sorrowful beasts already existed

in ancient times. Thousands of years ago, they came to Yong'an City in the south of China. This city was beset on four sides, facing sandstorms to the south and west, and humidity to the north and east – so the beasts settled in the north-east, becoming an isolated community that married off its attractive females to the highest bidders, splitting the proceeds forty-sixty with the local government. As our city acquired skyscrapers and elevated highways, they continued in their dilapidated estate, at peace with the world, placid and mild.

When I was at university, my professor told me, 'All beasts have a beastly nature. Please take care around them.'

I phoned and told him about my latest discoveries. 'Don't dig any further,' he said seriously. 'It won't do you any good.'

'I want to know how he died.'

My tutor sighed. 'Stubborn as ever. There are things it's better to forget.'

But I couldn't forget this: the night before graduation, my professor brought me to see his collection of beastly specimens, soaking in long vitrines, their faces so human. I remembered the male sorrowful beast. The green patch on his belly had been cut open. Inside were two rows of tightly packed teeth, and between these two rows, a gaping void. My tutor had said, 'That's his true mouth. His beastly mouth.'

I couldn't stop retching. I ran out of the lab, and never went back.

Every beast has a beastly nature. At the full moon, human children ought to stay at home.

My mother would say, 'The beasts all want to eat people, just as people eat them.'

Mutual destruction is the only way to survive. That's the circle of life. That's truth.

But scientists said they'd invented and put out a brand-new hormone that could completely suppress the beastly nature of female sorrowful beasts. Even at the full moon, they would no longer screech their birdlike cries.

They held clinical trials, and the results were undeniably successful. The drug was mass produced, with a hefty price tag – after all, the wives of rich men had someone to foot the bill. Charley was outraged at the time. 'This disrupts the ecological equilibrium!' he'd yelled, as his latest girlfriend gazed worshipfully at him.

I took a deep drag on my cigarette. It was easy to imagine a Yong'an many years from now with no beasts left, all of them dead from the hormones. Or else completely under control, stuffed full with humanity, passing between the skyscrapers, hopping in and out of lifts, dating and getting married, reproducing but stopping at one child, never mind if it was a boy or girl.

When that time came, surely all novelists would have hormone injections to turn us into computer programmers, and all zoologists would undergo surgery to become bus conductors. Everyone would give up their hollow pursuits, and there'd be no myths, no beasts, no history, no fantasy. The government would rattle along, printing money. Yong'an would truly become an international metropolis.

Therefore, historians of the future ought to thank the female beast Rain. She was allergic to the hormone shots, which turned her skin bright red, leaving her screeching non-stop. Most Yong'an residents saw the horrifying scene on TV: Rain's skin scarlet and almost transparent, the human foetus faintly visible through the bare skin of her belly, her hair flying wildly as she ran naked through the streets, the TV station's van careening after her.

People saw a terrified, tormented sorrowful beast, and just like the little beast said to me, she was smiling. Sorrowful beasts don't smile from joy, but only because of sadness, because of pain. Once they start, it's impossible to stop, until they die.

Her smile was so beautiful, even I wept for her. The whole city was captivated. As she sprinted, she shrieked like a bird. Old people said they'd die without regrets now, having lived to see the smile of a sorrowful beast.

She smiled down the entire length of Yanhe Street, then climbed the statue of the ancient hero in Victory Square. Her foetus stared helplessly through the translucent skin of her belly.

She let out a final, shattering cry, her smile as dazzling as the peach blossoms. Nearby witnesses said seeing her was like looking upon a goddess.

Then she died. Once sorrowful beasts smile, they die.

—

Production of the new hormone was brought to a sudden halt. The sorrowful beasts of Leye Estate went on a protest march, roaring as they paraded down the street. Humans ducked out of their way, terrified. The mayor came forward to speak. He offered his apologies, and arranged a funeral for Rain, the most lavish public ceremony ever seen.

On TV, her husband sobbed heart-rendingly, his shoulders heaving. A moving sight. Charley brought me to the funeral. Outside the ceremonial hall, we ran into Lefty and He Qi.

Lefty looked at me with a strange expression. She was even lovelier than ever, but so fragile, unsmiling, her expression pensive, her figure frail. He Qi clutched her hand tightly.

Not one of us said a word about Cloud. We nodded sombrely and went inside. Lefty wanted to see Rain's body. He Qi held her back, but she said, 'I want to take a last look, I didn't take good care of her.'

He Qi said, 'Don't go over there, it'll make you sad.'

But no one could have expected what happened next.

Lefty ran over like a madwoman, shoved the coffin lid open, and stared at the body inside. She reached out, as if to touch the body, but before making contact, she smiled.

It was a radiant smile, and everyone was momentarily enchanted. Charley, standing beside me, let out a meaningless exhalation, a typical man's grunt. Lefty was smiling, and now she couldn't stop. He Qi stumbled over to tug at her. 'You mustn't smile.' he murmured. 'She's dead, but don't smile!'

He wept, and still she smiled. He said, 'I love you so much, please don't leave me. It took so much for us to be together. Stop smiling!'

Still smiling, she let out a peal of proud, beautiful birdsong. Her voice rose up, startling everyone present.

Then she died.

And that was how the artist Lefty met her end.

—

In Yong'an City's Dolphin Bar, one often ran into the resident busybody Charley. His most recent gossip was of the artist Lefty and her sorrowful beast.

The way he told it, the government carried out an autopsy on her corpse, and in her faintly green belly, they found the teeth that hadn't yet broken down, and the half-digested remains of the real Lefty's body.

My professor phoned to scold me. 'I warned you not to dig any deeper.' Then he asked if he should come and see me, but I said there was no need.

Much later, I ran into He Qi at a party. He'd grown more feeble-looking. Pulling at my arm, he asked, 'You've written so many stories, you tell me, can humans and beasts love each other? Can they be together?'

I felt cold all over, and suddenly thought of the artist Lefty, or perhaps by then she was already the sorrowful beast Cloud, asking me sadly on the telephone, 'Can humans and beasts love each other? Is it possible?'

'I love He Qi,' she'd said.

I'd once thought I knew the whole story. I thought it was him and her. Who'd have guessed it was a tragedy of him and him? They'd thought they could be together, but in the end, it lasted no longer than flowers in a mirror, the moon reflected in water. It ended because her smile was so beautiful.

—

The sorrowful beasts live in the north-eastern quarter of Yong'an City. Guileless by nature, they prefer the cold. Since ancient times, no calamity has weakened them. At the full moon, the female beasts let out long mating calls, and the males hasten to them. There are fewer male sorrowful beasts than female, for on nights when the moon is full, a male is able to mate with a human woman, and at the moment of greatest pleasure, he opens his green belly-mouth wide and swallows her whole. He then takes on her likeness, slowly digesting her consciousness, finally becoming a new female beast. And so the species perpetuates, generation after generation.

These beasts are faithful, and only seek one mate in life. But they never smile. If they do, they die – hence their name.

JOYOUS BEASTS

Joyous beasts are an ancient breed; the god of thunder's steed was named Joyous. They only have a single gender, and their short stature makes them no different in appearance from a human child of six or seven, apart from a slightly longer left arm with five to seven claws at the wrist.

Joyous beasts love breakfast cereal and plain water, and dislike greasy, strong-tasting foods. They enjoy fantasy novels, and hate maths.

Joyous beasts are auspicious creatures. They live alone, and their movements are mysterious. Anyone who lays eyes on one is destined to prosper and rise above the herd. There are legends of emperors in ancient times encountering these beasts, hence their name, joyous.

The first sighting in Yong'an City was fifty years ago. A record of this incident can be found in the municipal library.

Five decades ago, a *Yong'an Chronicle* journalist snapped a picture of one such beast. In this colourised image, the tiny thing appears malnourished, with huge eyes, short hair, and a thick fringe. Its skin has been tinted a peculiar shade of pink, and its tracksuit is green. It looks panicked, standing at the edge of the frame, smiling with eyes that look like they're about to weep.

The reporter followed the beast around for half a month, noting its small appetite, feeding it cereal and plain water, and letting it read fantasy comic books. He recalled, 'It was very affectionate towards me, as if I was its dad.'

After the report came out, the beast vanished suddenly, and was never heard from again.

The journalist became an overnight sensation, and his career rocketed. Eventually, he became the mayor of Yong'an.

—

A week ago, the former mayor had died in his retirement home. He never married, and had no children. Among the possessions he left behind were three boxes of old books and clothes, and a savings account containing 1,700 yuan.

The story of the mayor and the joyous beast took

up an entire page of the *Yong'an Daily*, along with the old photograph from the *Chronicle*, and an advert for breast enhancement. The reverse side was full of classifieds: second-hand cars for cheap, young women seeking foreign men for English lessons, marriage proposals, houses for rent, furniture removals, cleaning services, missing persons, missing pets, all tightly crammed together in a bewildering array.

Among these there were a few lines about Li Chun, an old woman who'd been missing for some days now. No picture, just a description: short and slender, a mole beneath her right eye, doesn't speak much. If found please call this number, grateful reward promised.

I met my friend Charley at the Dolphin Bar. He smacked the paper down on the table and yelled, 'Did you see this? They put my number on this crappy ad! How would you even find anyone with a description like that? My goddamn phone's been ringing off the hook since seven this morning!'

Someone laughed, 'Hey, Charley, I bet someone's pranking you – must be because you're so annoying.'

I sat across from him, smoking, my head throbbing painfully. 'What paper is that?'

And that's how I saw the picture of the joyous beast.

The creature looked wholesome and innocent. It was smiling, but terror lurked in its eyes; I stared at it for a long time. I went to the municipal library the next day, but didn't find out much more. In fifty years, there'd only been this one joyous beast, and no one had set eyes on it but the late former mayor.

And now, me.

—

Yong'an City has countless beasts, some identical to human beings, some truly monstrous. At university, I'd seen many pictures of them in my professor's office, even perspective-free images of long-extinct species from antiquity. Yet none ever stirred me as much as this one. The joyous beast in the photograph looked directly at the camera, terrified yet smiling, strangely like myself.

I called my professor and asked if he had any stories. 'You know the legends, don't you? I remember them being on our syllabus.'

He said, 'Yes, they're bizarre and dangerous, and we still study them today. Even though no one can say for sure whether they actually exist.'

'But that picture in the morning paper—'

'Didn't show its wrist, let alone any claws! That photograph proves nothing.'

I snapped, 'You've lost your edge! There was a time when you'd have hunted it down.'

'That's right, you've aggravated me into old age!'

I put down the phone grumpily.

Of course, there was someone in a worse mood than me: Charley was now a de facto private eye, searching for Li Chun. Calls came in constantly with accounts of old women at the train station, by Splendid River, at Heavenly Beauty Mall, even at Municipal High School Number Two. Charley was flung around like a spinning top, but it was always a case of mistaken identity. 'I hope it doesn't take me long to return her to the bosom of her family,' he said to me on the phone. 'I'm tired of this nonsense.'

I laughed and said, 'Why not just change your phone number?' As soon as the words left my mouth, I knew they shouldn't have. Charley sneered, 'We've been friends for more than ten years, and you get more naïve by the day.'

Neither of us said anything for a while. There are some sore spots no one should prod.

I thought about how Charley didn't even need to change his number. A call to his pals at the newspaper would sort out the misunderstanding, but of course he'd never do that. He was set on finding this stranger and returning her home.

I said, 'Charley, you're too good-hearted.'

He chuckled, and hung up.

I don't know when people stopped saying good-bye. Anything to cut down on phone bills.

I dreamed of the joyous beast that night. It stood there, smiling at me, as tiny as a human child. Its enormous eyes bored straight into me, and it said nothing, contorting its face into such a horrifying expression that I woke up screaming in fear.

———

I slept badly all night. The next morning, I woke unusually early. Heading out in search of breakfast, I met one of the fabled bird-sellers: a middle-aged woman with sallow skin and dry hair, gnawing at a fried dough stick, sidling over to whisper, 'Want a bird, miss?'

I looked at her, and something in my brain twitched so I said yes.

The woman took me to look at her birds. I couldn't help thinking how, more than thirty years ago, Yong'an was full of these creatures: thrushes, magpies, crows, cranes, wild geese, sparrows, any kind you could want, migratory or not, filling the air with their chirps. Then the mysterious massacre of the birds began. First it was the academics who disseminated papers claiming that birds spread all kinds of deadly diseases, that they caused noise pollution, that they reduced the supply of staple foods. Next, the local government got involved, launching a campaign to kill them with guns or nets, burning or burying their bodies, tearing apart their nests and smashing their eggs. Champion bird-eliminators were lauded, and political leaders made speeches of such gravity that no one could treat this as a joke. From then on, birds vanished from Yong'an, at least as far as anyone could see. If any survived, they didn't dare make a peep. Now and then, bird-sellers showed up from the countryside, and were treated by the authorities as a serious threat, as bad as porn vendors. They'd come over and ask, 'Hey, want a bird?' – or sometimes, 'How about a nature film?'

This may sound comical, but as I said, the local government took it very seriously, and sent out many documents covered in bright red official stamps. No one dared to laugh about it. Even when the leader of the bird-elimination campaign passed away, those who came after him honoured his memory by continuing to arrest bird-sellers.

Which is why, when this woman handed me a bird, I didn't even check to see what breed it was. She said thirty yuan, and I paid up.

Then I asked, 'What kind of bird is it, Auntie?'
She replied, 'A good bird.'

It was grey, with a red beak, maintaining a very
unbirdlike silence, except when it shrieked and shook
its head, prancing around in its cage. I named it Little
Grey.

My professor, with the instincts of a hunting dog,
phoned me. After a bit of small talk, he said, 'So
you've got a bird now.'

I said yes, and he launched into a rant about how I
was sure to get found out and fined a huge sum. Then
he said, 'Come by in a few days, I have some good
bird food to give you.'

He asked if I'd made any progress with the joyous
beast.

I said no.

'I've found a connection,' he said. 'We can go visit
the former mayor's nursing home tomorrow.'

I said, 'So you're rejuvenated.'

He laughed icily. 'Meet me at the usual place,
nine-thirty tomorrow.'

—

I waited half an hour but he never came. Eventually,
a young man showed up, looking like a student. 'The
professor sent me,' he said. 'He's busy.' A bright-eyed,

baby-faced boy in a checked shirt. Blushing, he said, 'I've read your novels.'

After taking my leave, I got the 378 bus to the retirement home on Shepherd's Hill. As we zoomed along the airport expressway, I could hear the rumble of planes landing and taking off in the distance. Soon they would soar like phoenixes, heading to distant places.

The retirement home was lovely, a series of grey-white houses in a courtyard full of camphor, birch, and eucalyptus trees, burgeoning flower beds by the entrance. It was gardenia season, and the soft snow-white blossoms filled the garden with their scent.

Nursing Aide Number 73 brought me to the former mayor's former rooms, 104. 'They've been empty since the old man passed,' he said. 'No one's touched anything, it's all just as it was.'

I went in. It was so tidy, it felt as if no one had ever been in here. The newspaper headlines praising the mayor's integrity and honesty flashed before my eyes, as if on a cinema screen. The outer room had a coffee table, three cane chairs and a 29-inch TV. Further in was his bedroom. His bookshelves took up more space than his wardrobe. Beyond that was an airwell, then a kitchen and bathroom. The standard layout of an old-fashioned home.

I asked Number 73, 'Did the mayor leave anything else behind?'

He glared at me. 'Didn't you read the papers? Two boxes of books and one of clothes, nothing else.'

The walls were painted stark white. When they caught the sun, it was momentarily blinding. I said, 'I'm surprised the mayor didn't get dazzled, looking at these all day.'

The aide said, 'Who the hell is so bored they stare at walls all day?'

As I looked around, he followed behind me, his face completely blank. I silently cursed my professor about a hundred and fifty times, then got out my cigarettes and offered Number 73 one: 'Smoke?' He said no, so I lit one myself, sucked deeply on it, smiled beguilingly at the guy, and said goodbye.

It was three in the afternoon. Number 73 walked the length of the facility with me. Identical grey-white houses, all numbered, flashed past, silent as an abandoned town. He bid me farewell, and vigorously shoved the gate shut.

I headed for the Dolphin Bar and told Charley all about my visit. 'It was so clean,' I said. 'So clean.' Charley sat across from me guzzling beer and eating peanuts. He said, 'Do you believe in that sort of cleanliness? The tidiest room still accumulates dust, unless you sweep it every day.'

His phone started ringing again.

———

We spotted Li Chun in front of Galaxy Cinema, the neon lights behind her radiant as a stage. She was sitting on the steps, shrunken as a child, her head hung low so we couldn't see her expression, white hair above a red satin blouse.

The snack shop owner who'd summoned us said, 'She's been there a few hours. I asked for her name, and when she said Li Chun, I phoned you.'

She looked up when we walked towards her. Her eyes were deep black and enormous. There was sadness in the way she looked at me, but then she smiled. There was a mole beneath her right eye.

She was very old, and her skin covered in wrinkles, but you could tell she'd once been beautiful. Her eyes were bright, her nose well-formed, and the lines of her face very delicate.

'Are you Li Chun?' we asked. She looked at us a little curiously, but didn't deny it.

Charley said, 'Your family's searching for you. Where's your home? I'll take you back.'

'Who are you?' she said.

'I'm the unlucky bastard whose number was

published,' he snapped.

She smiled at him. 'All right, take me home.'

The snack shop owner beamed as if he'd won the lottery. Li Chun pulled out her purse, handed five hundred yuan to the man, and said, 'Thank you.'

He took the money and waltzed away. All he'd seen were the banknotes, but Charley and I had both caught a glimpse of Li Chun's wrist: pale, scrawny, and sporting six bony spurs, like infant teeth. Her left wrist.

I said, 'You're not human.'

She said, 'That's right, I'm a joyous beast.'

Her eyes met mine and she smiled, just the same as the little beast in the photograph. A chill shot down my spine.

—

We took Li Chun home. She lived in the family compound of People's Hospital Number Six. I asked, 'Are you a doctor?'

'Yes, traditional medicine.'

We dropped by her flat. Her living room was spotless; pink drapes and a little bar counter. 'Do you live alone?' asked Charley.

'I never married,' said Li Chun.

She asked if we'd like a drink, and went to get

some glasses. I watched closely, and sure enough, her left arm was a little longer than her right. We sat down, and she poured us a drink, her movements like a graceful dance.

Charley took a sip, looking anxious. This was probably his first real encounter with a beast.

He said, 'About that phone number...'

'It was a mistake,' said Li Chun, smiling. 'His number has a 6 at the end, yours a 9.'

'Whose?' I asked.

'He's not with us any more,' she said.

I had no interest in her love story, so I plunged ahead to the main point. 'Do you know the joyous beast in this picture?'

'Yes,' said Li Chun, elegantly raising her glass to her lips. 'That's me.'

Her eyes were pitch-black as she stared at me. She looked exactly like an elderly human being. Fifty years ago, she'd still been a young beast.

'I thought joyous beasts never stopped looking like children, and had no gender,' I muttered.

She chuckled. 'People know far too little about joyous beasts.'

She was right. We have barely any knowledge, but are conceited enough to fill books with our ignorance anyway. Countless people make a living in this way, bluffing their way into wealth and respectability. Yet no one understands the life of a beast: how they're born, how they die, how they think of humans, how they survive.

Perhaps that's why my brain refused to connect the young beast in the picture with this elderly one. Yet even in her old age, her eyes hadn't changed one bit. I asked casually, 'How long do joyous beasts live?'

'We're immortal,' she said.

I was exhausted. Charley brought me home and poured me a glass of milk, then put me to bed like a big brother. I murmured drowsily, 'Don't forget to feed my bird.' He tweaked my nose and said, 'Sure.'

We had taken different routes to the same destination. He'd been after Li Chun while I tracked down the joyous beast. Who'd have thought they were the same?

That night I dreamed again of the joyous beast, still looking childlike, the terror in her eyes even greater than before. All of a sudden, she let out a shrill, beastly cry, exactly like a bird call.

I was startled awake, but the noise continued. It was my own bird, chirping away like a lunatic.

I rushed into the living room and saw the little thing hopping about in its cage, squawking wildly. Dashing over in a panic, I smelled the alcohol fumes from its trough. Stupid Charley – he'd filled it with clear liquor by mistake.

Suppressing the impulse to phone and yell at him, I poured away the liquor and replaced it with water, then put a black cloth over the cage. I tried to get back to sleep, but couldn't.

I sat by the window, hugging a cushion and smoking. Looking down, I noticed with a start that the woods outside our city were growing, sending out rapid tendrils that engulfed our buildings, blocking all light so there was just the moon and a thick layer of cloud. The sky was so far away, and just like ancient times, there was no longer any town, no people, just beasts scampering through the woods, clutching and biting, killing each other, mating and neglecting their offspring.

Out of nowhere, a bird rose into the air, or maybe it was many birds, I can't remember, because it – or they – were so beautiful: an elongated body and exquisite movements, feathers as pale and radiant as a phoenix, all the colours of the world in those wings, soaring over Yong'an Forest, letting out a piercing cry, unbearably sad, circling the city once, then disappearing into the clouds.

My own bird continued cawing like a mad thing.

Three minutes later, my professor called in a

frenzy. 'Did you see the bird? I'm serious! That wasn't just any bird – I'm sure it was some kind of beast.'

So that was no hallucination. I couldn't help laughing.

—

The next day, the story made the front pages of Yong'an's newspapers, along with a blurry photograph. It turned out there were plenty of insomniacs in the city, hence no shortage of witnesses. Old people wept for the cameras, and one elderly woman said she'd been a little girl the last time she'd seen anything this miraculous. Others insisted the creature must be a phoenix, the sacred bird of legend. People were talking about it all day long.

At nightfall, I went to the Dolphin Bar, where I heard the young punk next to me swilling his beer and bragging that he'd seen a bird like that long before today, although he hadn't thought it was real.

I turned to see what he looked like but accidentally met his eye, so had to smile awkwardly at him.

A few minutes later, he came over, bought me a drink, and said, 'I've seen you before.'

I looked down, but he stubbornly insisted, 'No, I have. Where was it?'

He took out his cigarettes and tilted them towards

me. 'Smoke?'

'No, thanks.'

He smiled and said, 'I remember you now, you came to the retirement home!'

'Oh! And you're Number 73!'

We both burst out laughing.

He had a few drinks with me, even though he was probably already drunk. Leaning close, reeking of alcohol, he told me about the former mayor.

'The old man was always a bit strange. Just hid in his room, painting away.' Lowering his voice mysteriously, he went on, 'And do you know what he was painting? A bird! The one from last night. One and the same!'

I narrowed my eyes, and decided to ignore this drunken man. I recalled the bright sunlight, those dazzling white walls. To think there'd been such a gorgeous bird behind them.

—

I phoned my professor and told him everything. He asked if I'd visited the beast again. I said, 'No, I don't like disturbing people.' He said, 'That's right, I remember that about you.' Neither of us said anything for a while, then he said, 'Come out for dinner tomorrow, it's almost your birthday.'

I laughed and said, 'All right.'

He stood me up again. I waited an hour at the hotel restaurant, until the same boyish student turned up. 'The professor's busy,' he said. 'He told me to give you this.'

Uncertain if I should be amused or angry, I opened the envelope and found a photograph.

The man in the picture wasn't my professor. He had a high nose and wore glasses, and looked a little dull-witted. The woman next to him was short and skinny, with delicate features and pitch-black eyes, boring right into me. It was winter, and they were both swaddled up in the snow. It was an old photograph, the people in it still young.

My annoyance dissipated. 'Fine, since you're here, I'll buy you dinner.'

He blushed and said, 'All right.'

We had a delicious meal, and polished off the vintage red wine I'd ordered specially. I said, 'So what's been happening at the university?'

He said, 'We've been researching joyous beasts. It's strange, the professor makes us go to the municipal archives every day, and we trawl through all the old papers, but I have no idea what they have to do with anything.'

I broke into a cold sweat, and suddenly felt much

less drunk. My professor hadn't changed. Pulling out the photo again, I asked the boy, 'Who's this man?'

'The former Yong'an mayor,' he said. 'The professor said you'd be sure to recognise him.'

I looked again, and yes, now I could tell it was him. The woman, those eyes – that was Li Chun, the joyous beast.

It was definitely her, staring straight at me and smiling. She was fully grown in the picture, and as I'd expected, very beautiful.

—

I arranged to meet Charley and asked him what happened when he dialled his own number with the final digit changed from 9 to 6 – was it the former mayor's line? He busied himself with sending a text message and said, 'How would I know?'

'Don't pretend, you're such a busybody, of course you tried the number.'

He grinned sheepishly, and said, yes, he had, and sure enough, it was a love story.

I hadn't asked further after the beast said, 'He's not with us any more,' but I'd already had an inkling.

He was still young then, just a reporter, when he saw the young beast through his camera lens and came to fall in love with her. Why did they part and grow old alone? No one knew. A love story.

But he'd put out a classified ad wanting to know where she was, this taciturn beast with a mole under her eye. She'd seen the ad, and also his obituary on the other side of the page. A love story.

Just a love story. Forget it.

We sat there smoking. A classic love story. Fifty years. Since then, there'd been earthquakes, wars, even that ridiculous campaign to get rid of all the birds. I laughed, then started coughing.

When I shut my eyes, I could see through the camera's lens. The sunlight in the distance. The little beast stood in her tracksuit, aslant with desire and weakness, so eager to smile for him. Her eyes were pitch-black and enormous, gleaming, and there was terror in her expression. The sun reflected off her face as brightly as those white walls.

Abruptly, I shivered, and then again.

Clutching Charley's hand, I said, 'That day's paper – where is it?'

He'd tossed it aside at the Dolphin Bar. We hurried there and found it. I hadn't imagined it – for all that it had been colourised that strange shade of pink, the little beast's skin was clear and unblemished.

There was no mole beneath her right eye.

That wasn't all, I realised belatedly. In the

photograph my professor sent me, the woman was also mole-free.

I showed Charley the picture and asked who he thought she was.

'A hot chick.'

'Is it Li Chun?'

'No.'

'Why not?'

He took a slow drag on his cigarette and frowned. 'Are you stupid? This woman must be at least twenty years older than Li Chun. Didn't you see the date? Fifty years ago, Li Chun was still a child.'

I grabbed the picture back and stared in consternation. There was the date, printed clearly on the bottom right corner. The joyous beast would still have been childlike, genderless.

We went over to Li Chun's place immediately, only to find it empty. Charley banged at the door despairingly, until the old man next door came out in a pair of white shorts, his skin sagging like a giant beanbag. 'Are you looking for Li Chun? She's gone. A bunch of people came a few days ago, and took away all her things. I've always thought there was something wrong with her,' he said conspiratorially. 'She wasn't like a regular person. I've been her neighbour for thirty years, yet we barely spoke.'

It was a tragedy. She was just a beast, but now we'd lost her, no one would ever find out about her upbringing, or what had happened next. Joyous beasts are solitary and their movements mysterious. You almost never encounter one.

Charley had his wits about him more than I did. He reached into my bag and pulled out the photograph. 'Do you know these people?'

The old man squinted. 'That woman looks a lot like Li Chun when she was young, and the man, isn't that the former mayor? Is Li Chun related to them?'

Startled, I snatched the picture back, said a hasty goodbye, and dragged Charley away with me.

—

I walked home alone that night, working my way through many cigarettes. We'd got the story wrong, but there must surely be other stories. The former mayor was dead, this other woman or beast had yet to show herself, and then there was the joyous beast Li Chun. But I'd lost the scent.

I was almost certain that the photograph showed another little beast.

Nights are so dark in Yong'an. After sundown, illusory trees sprout from the earth, crackling as they grow, reaching up to the clouds, blossoming into the beguiling memories of beasts. Distantly, indistinctly, something cries out.

I inhaled so deeply on my cigarette that I choked and started coughing. Squatting in the small park I walked through all the time, I imagined the strange young beast from the picture. Those fearful, smiling eyes. This was a ghost, I realised with clarity. The beast was dead, which was why it could appear to me. Yong'an is a city in which spirits, beasts and humans mingle, brushing shoulders in the street, falling in love, even having children. No one dies a good death.

My phone rang.

It was my professor. I answered, but didn't say anything. He sighed. 'Don't cry, I'm coming to you now. The joyous beast is gone.'

'I know,' I said, my voice heavy.

'Come to the lab tomorrow,' he said.

'All right,' I said.

—

I couldn't wait till the next day, but drove to the university right away, taking the route I knew so well back to the lab. I got my keys out – I knew he'd never changed the locks – and opened the door.

I clicked the switch, and when the lights came on, the traces of my guilt evaporated. The room was scattered with stuff, as if it had been ransacked. It all looked familiar. I knew right away these were Li Chun's possessions. I ought to have guessed.

There was a stack of documents on the desk, clearly a case file. On the cover of the folder next to them: 'Joyous Beast 001'.

These were also Li Chun's: letters that had never been sent, describing events from many years ago, like an ancient legend. Some were addressed to a man. 'I feel like I'm falling in love with you, so I don't want to leave. This is torture, and you won't see me, but I don't want to leave. Besides, I never meant to hurt anyone.' Just that, among her meagre possessions. A hideous scrawl, like a child who'd only just learnt to write.

There were photographs too. One was in a garden, beneath bright sunlight. She was still young, scrawny but beautiful, standing alone, smiling in confusion.

The former mayor's things were here too, in a bag marked with his name. I saw the picture first: the mayor as a young man, still a reporter, camera round his neck. The woman from the other photo was here too, and between them, holding their hands, a beaming girl of five or six. She had a mole beneath her eye.

The next item was a letter to his wife. 'She's no longer our daughter, she's become a monster. Kill her, right away, before I get back. Kill her!'

Then there were records of a police investigation, covered in official stamps. A break-in at the newspaper's staff lodgings on such-and-such a date. A woman hacked to death, her daughter missing. The man had light injuries and remained unconscious. Speed was of the essence, and so on. But the report was inconclusive. The case remained a stain on the reputation of the police, and no one knew what had really happened.

There was also some material about the eradication of the birds, probably confidential. This was from when the man was mayor, a draft memo claiming birds could eat people, and had to be driven out of Yong'an.

Finally, there were scans of some drawings, so blurry from age that they were hard to make out.

The first showed the phoenix-like bird I'd seen, unbelievably graceful, neck twisted, eyes gleaming black.

The next was of the other beast, the one from the photograph, smiling in the sun, very thin, almost skin and bones. Her eyes were still bright, still fearful.

The last picture was the little beast again, now dead, laid out on a balcony. Its left arm was stretched up high, the seven spurs on its wrist clearly visible, jagged as tree branches. Its eyes were shut, its right hand on its chest, clenched tightly as if in pain. The left arm was at least three times longer than the right, and rose oddly towards the sky – though this was a sketch, so rough I wondered how much of it was my imagination.

I went over to the specimen cabinet, where I found a new addition: a shrivelled arm in a jar. It was very thin, with six claws at the pale wrist. The arm had been cut open, and was completely hollow inside, all the flesh eaten clean away.

When I got home that night, I looked at myself in the mirrored lift, and saw terror in my eyes. I thought of the beast inside Li Chun's body, eating its lover's flesh-and-blood child, day after day, prolonging the meal as much as possible, not wanting to leave this body connected to him. It waited, and ate a little; ate a little, and waited. All in all, this devouring took fifty years. When it left, and soared over the city, it recalled their first meeting, how he'd treated it like his own daughter, how he'd taken that photograph, murmuring, 'Come on, smile.' The beast smiled, but the little girl who was being eaten from the inside looked fearful. My own face gleamed back at me from the lift doors, a pair of black eyes, tears streaming.

I opened my front door and saw that my bird had

died. Its wings were dry and rigid, no longer moving.

—

The joyous beast is an auspicious one. It takes the form of a phoenix, speaks human languages, and is loyal by nature. The joyous beast cannot survive long on its own, and spends most of its existence as a parasite in a human host. It loves to feed on children. When everything in the body has been eaten — the organs, the muscles, the brain, the blood — it leaves through the long left arm, transforming into an enormous bird, a creature of awesome beauty that only lives a single night.

The joyous beast reproduces through death. A feather from its head finds a new body to latch on to, and once lodged there, it will gestate a new being.

From death into life, and so for thousands of years. The joyous beasts are immortal.

SACRIFICIAL BEASTS

Sacrificial beasts are melancholy by nature, drawn to high places and low temperatures. In the distant past, they could be found on mountain peaks. They are tall and dark-skinned, with pale blue eyes and thin lips. Their earlobes hang low, and have a sawtoothed edge. In all other respects, they are like regular people.

The males of the species speak no human languages, and are prone to fighting. The females, for their part, are warm-natured and often multilingual. Their speaking voices are mellifluous, and their singing is like the music of the celestial spheres. Each female takes two or three mates, who fight each other for her amusement.

These beasts live in tribes. They are healthy, heal quickly, and do not injure easily. Yet they also love to destroy each other, over and over, until death. Hence their name, sacrificial.

The males die most frequently due to their

pugnacious natures, the females less so.

As a result, since ancient times, the numbers of sacrificial beasts have not stopped falling, and they have long since been endangered. Although humans have set up nature reserves and protection zones, these don't prevent the beasts from destroying one another. There are also breeding programmes in place, but the newborns often refuse sustenance and die soon after.

In Cloudtop Towers, the tallest building in Yong'an, the fiftieth to sixtieth floors were a sanctuary for these beasts, housing fifty-six of them. Yong'an was the world's biggest centre for sacrificial beast research, and drew scholars from all over. Their annual conference alone did much for the city's economy.

Sacrificial beasts were at one time considered the city's mascots, until they were replaced for being too depressing. Even so, schoolchildren showed up at Cloudtop Towers every weekend to visit the beasts.

In order to keep them from killing one another, the beasts were housed in individual enclosures, each with the facilities of a luxury flat. And yet the carnage continued, particularly during the full moon. Scientists kept the beasts tied to their beds and blindfolded during this time, playing upbeat rock music or TV comedies to get them through the slump.

And still the population continued to dwindle.

Exacerbating the situation, their libidos also declined, making breeding impossible. Scientists racked their brains for a solution, while the government launched a campaign to 'Save the Final Beast' by any means possible, urging the public to give generously, organising for celebrities to perform and meet with them.

The death of each sacrificial beast was headline news, causing young women throughout the city to shed tears. Births were even more of an occasion. With each one, a holiday was proclaimed in Yong'an City to wish the young beast a long life of good fortune. The mother was fêted too, with a banquet held in her honour. Like any heroine of the people, she was asked to give speeches and interviews.

Yesterday, another sacrificial beast died.

—

My niece Lucia, my cousin's daughter, happened to be on an outing to Cloudtop Towers. She'd been all excited to meet the beasts, but upon returning her little face was chalk-white from fear. She refused to eat when she got home, and sobbed non-stop while demanding to see her strange aunt who wrote stories. My cousin and her husband, who could never say no to their daughter, phoned me right away to ask if I'd come persuade Lucia to eat her dinner.

I'd been at the Dolphin Bar waiting for a performance to start: a monkey from the south was going to turn somersaults for us. Now I had to call a taxi to rush to their home and cheer up their little darling. Charley laughed at me for not having a mind of my own.

I said, 'Charley, you're too used to being alone. You don't understand family life.'

Beastly families were a mystery to me, but I genuinely felt that when it came to humans, families were a great institution. Like the roots of a tree, they gave you life and sustained you, and even when you died, you stayed rooted.

Lucia didn't understand any of this – she was still a little girl. When she saw me, she howled and flung herself into my embrace. 'Auntie,' she sobbed. My heart shattered, and I quickly produced the Black Forest gâteau I'd brought to cheer her up. She loved me, and I loved her too.

She said, 'I saw it die, you know.'

I held her little head and murmured as tenderly as I could, 'Everything that lives must die.'

She didn't seem to understand. 'But if we all die, who's going to go to work, who's going to cook dinner?'

I had to laugh, but remembered feeling the same

sorrow when I was younger, and telling my mother, 'One day we'll all be dead and the streets will be empty. Who's going to sweep them? It's so scary.'

My mother had smiled and said, 'We'll be dead, but new people will arrive. Back to the beginning, on and on. As for us, we'll meet again in the distance, perhaps as strangers who once brushed past each other. That's destiny.'

For the next half hour, I became a monkey – telling jokes and turning somersaults. Finally, Lucia cheered up. She was a child, after all, and had already forgotten about the beast's death. She gobbled down her dinner, grumbling to my cousin that the beef was tough, and that there wasn't enough variety in the dessert selection.

My cousin came downstairs with me. In the lift, I asked, 'How did the beast die?'

She furrowed her brows and said, 'It sounded horrible. Apparently it sliced its belly open with a dinner knife, spilling its guts all over the floor. Just to make sure, it sliced up each intestine into little pieces. They don't die easily.' She sighed. 'Yet it wanted so badly to die.'

No wonder Lucia had been crying. Hearing this story, I'd all but fainted. And yet, looking at it rationally, the death of every sacrificial beast was equally tragic. Their life force was just too strong. Only the most vicious methods could destroy them.

—

This was the sixth sacrificial beast to die that year. Despite the many protections, with every eventuality thought of, we still lost one every month, until it came to feel like a regular event. When the moon was full, a sacrificial beast would die, and there was no way around it. Their ends were all as gruesome as something from a horror film. Never mind sliced intestines, one slit its throat with so much force that only a flap of skin at the back of its neck kept its head attached. Another jumped from the roof of Cloudtop Towers, smearing the pavement below with red goo. And other ways too, but never mind that for now.

The newspaper reports were often printed in red on black: 'Sacrificial Beast Dies, Only XX Still Alive!!!' There were always countless exclamation marks, and the number got smaller each time.

When it came to the methods of death, journalists heaped on the adjectives, but even described plainly they would have been sensational. They ran pixelated photographs, but as with human nudity, concealment served merely to titillate. The whole city went mad, fully revealing the depths of its perversion.

Some young people set up a sacrificial beast society to mimic the deaths. Parents were terrified. In January, a bunch of kids jumped from tall buildings, while February saw a spike in hangings, slit throats in March, and knives through the heart in April. Which brought us to the present moment, and it didn't take a genius to figure out that this month would see a rise in disembowelments. The sacrificial beasts were trendsetters in the world of suicide, just like when fashion magazines predict that black will be the hottest colour of the fall/winter season or that goths will be back in style, no rhyme or reason to it.

Yet before a single human had ripped out their guts, the news arrived: the sacrificial beasts were almost extinct anyway, and in light of the negative effect they were having on society, the remainder of the species would be exterminated, once and for all.

The city was stunned.

But entertainment news is explosive by nature, and the next day brought an even more shocking headline: two sacrificial beasts had fled, one male and one female.

—

As usual, Charley was adorably indifferent to what was happening around him. The next day, he brought his new girlfriend to meet me as we'd planned. In the wavering light of the Dolphin Bar, the pair of them looked like ghosts. Charley introduced us. 'This is Ru Ru.' Ru Ru had a little face, and long hair that reached her waist. She shook my hand and I smiled. 'Charley doesn't usually have such good taste.'

I hit it off with Ru Ru right away, and we started whispering to each other. She had a lovely voice, and the eyes of an infant: enormous dark pupils, like my niece Lucia. Feeling well-disposed towards her, I asked, 'How did you and Charley meet?'

'We come from the same town.'

'Oh, really?' I was curious. I'd been friends with Charley for many years, yet knew almost nothing about him. He never changed his phone number, which made me think he had an ex from long ago whom he hoped would find her way back to him some day. That was just a guess, though. No one actually knew.

We were city people, after all, and didn't ask too many questions.

We drank all evening, until Charley was smashed enough to ask, 'Do you know why I'm always changing girlfriends?'

'Because you're a pervert,' I said, fobbing him off.

'No, I'm torturing himself. I'm scared to be alone,

but when I'm part of a couple, the suffering of loneliness feels like the better option. Terrible life, glorious death. As exciting as a movie.'

'You're very noble, using your life to entertain the masses.' I rolled my eyes at him.

'You don't understand,' he said. 'We're not the same.'

I rolled my eyes again, and went back to my drink. 'Want a cigarette?' I asked him.

'Sure,' he said, taking Ru Ru's hand with infinite tenderness.

You can be a born actor, but that means everyone's watching you perform, and they laugh at you when you display emotion. If you can see all the way into the depths of truth but you just play the fool, that's ridiculous. And if you're completely unaware, even funnier.

—

Lucia phoned me. 'Auntie, the newspaper said they're going to kill the sacrificial beasts.'

'Yes,' I said, 'But grown-ups are always talking nonsense, you shouldn't believe them.'

The little girl was silent for a long time, then solemnly blurted out, 'He doesn't want to die.'

'Huh?' I said stupidly. Young people's minds moved

too quickly for me.

'The male beast,' she explained. 'Auntie, you write lots of stories about beasts, don't you? I understand them too. Even if they don't speak our language, they look a lot like us, and I can tell from their eyes what they're saying. He's telling me he doesn't want to die. All the while he's crying and bleeding...'

'Stop it.' I wished I could hug her through the telephone line. 'Don't let your imagination run away with you.'

'I'm not.' She sounded stubborn, just like me at her age. 'It really is like that, I know they don't want to die, poor things.'

I hung up, and sat thinking about what she'd said. When did the sacrificial beasts start killing themselves? Ten, twenty thousand years ago?

Sacrificial beasts had been around since the dawn of mankind, and they kept dying. How many years had it been? How many more of them must there once have been?

But could it be that they did not want to die? I ran Lucia's words through my mind again and again, until finally I had to smile.

Children are like that. They think life is as beautiful as a flower. But Lucia would grow up, and come to understand that sometimes living feels like chewing on wax. And so you let go. The more resilient life is, the more you want to destroy it, raze it to the ground, put on a show, all guns blazing, what joy.

The latest government tally was reported on TV: in January, a male beast jumped to his death, and so did twenty-three humans; in February, a male beast tied his hands together and hanged himself, and thirty-five people followed suit; in March, a male beast slit his throat… And so on, up to June, and the male beast Lucia saw ripping his belly open.

All the deceased were males. They couldn't speak. We couldn't understand.

Lucia had said, 'You don't understand, but I do. He doesn't want to die.'

All of a sudden, I broke into a cold sweat.

—

I had no choice but to phone my professor and ask, 'Did you know about the plan to kill off the sacrificial beasts?'

'Yes,' he said.

Just that one word, so casually tossed out. It enraged me. As a well-known zoologist, he'd probably been asked to join the planning committee long ago.

I said, 'Stop pretending you're so innocent.'

Unmoved, he went on, 'The males will be killed first, starting next month. The females are docile and speak human languages, they can wait a few months. And the cubs will be fed a slow-acting poison, also next month.'

'That's cruel,' I said.

'It's natural selection, survival of the fittest. Anyway, they're just beasts, not humans.'

'Yes, but their faces are the same as ours.' This was my Achilles heel, the reason I hadn't been able to complete my training as a zoologist, the reason I had ended up with the laughable, shameful profession of a novelist instead.

—

I met the tall man in the Dolphin Bar. He was standing at the entrance looking in. The lights were dim, but I could make out the outline of his attractive features.

I was sobbing when he came inside, half-drunk and thinking about the past. Still weeping, I crashed right into him.

He held me up, sorrow coming over his face. When he looked at me, his eyes were pure as a child's, baby blue.

'Are you looking for someone?' I asked.

He smiled but said nothing.

I walked away, and he followed. So I stopped and said, 'What do you want?' He came closer and took my hand in his enormous one. His palm was warm and dry. He pulled me into his embrace, and held my fingers to his ear: a sawtoothed edge.

Jagged earlobes. Blue eyes. Thin lips. A smile flickered across them as he stared at me.

A sacrificial beast.

He must have escaped. A male beast. Had he come looking for me? Why? But he couldn't answer my questions.

I brought him home.

In my flat, I fed him milk. He obediently lowered his head to lap at it, looking up now and then to smile at me again. At these moments, he reminded me of the first boy I fell in love with, who'd walk me home from school and stand at my doorway smiling silently at me, his eyes telling me he wanted a kiss.

And so I kissed him.

In a fog, I kissed the beast. His lips were icy-cold and moist, and his tongue was forked like a snake's.

I screamed in fright and pushed him away, covering my mouth. He looked at me, all innocence. His eyes were doting and helpless. How pathetic humanity is.

He parted his lips and let me look at his tongue. The split was clearly not natural, the wound still gory. Someone had sliced it in two.

Male beasts speak no human languages.

His tongue had been cut right down the middle. He hadn't died because his life force was so resilient, because he was a sacrificial beast.

Still in shock, I wanted to ask so many things, but he couldn't answer, and I didn't know how to put my questions into words.

He looked at me, brooding. Then, abruptly, he leaned across and kissed me. Like a snake, he was ice-cold and damp. I couldn't move.

At that moment, I decided to tame him.

—

We lay next to each other. His body was criss-crossed with scars, but he was warm, and wrapped me in his arms. His heat, like my mother's, soothed me to sleep. No words, a human and a beast. I clutched him like a drowning woman and drifted off peacefully.

I was still asleep when Charley called, and had to grope blearily for the phone. He asked, 'Are you with someone?'

I said no. It wasn't a lie, at least not a conscious one – he wasn't human, after all.

He wouldn't let it go. 'Really?'

'Yes, really.'

'You're lying.'

Ru Ru snatched the phone from him, sounding agitated. 'He's with you, isn't he? Don't move, we'll be right there.'

'We're downstairs,' Charley added.

The male beast next to me, scarred and drowsing, was startled awake by these words. His eyes filled with terror, and he pushed me aside. Huddling by the window, he let out a low howl.

I had no idea what was going on, but already there was a knocking at the door, as if the secret police had arrived.

I opened the door and he stormed in, Ru Ru right behind him. Seeing her by daylight, I noticed that her eyes were blue and her skin was dark. Beautiful as ever. She made straight for the bedroom and tugged at the male beast, murmuring gently, 'Why did you run away again? Come back with me, I've been looking all over for you. You aren't afraid to die, are you?'

I hovered by the doorway. Charley refused to meet my eye, just sat there smoking.

Very good, Charley. Dating beasts as well as humans, how open-minded of you.

We all sat down and formally introduced ourselves.

The male beast was named Fei Fei. 'He's my husband,' Ru Ru said.

I made everyone coffee, and put some toast on as well. Would they like peanut butter or apple jam? The perfect hostess. Then the beasts left, and Charley turned to me, eyes glistening. 'Did you…?'

'We didn't do anything,' I swiftly replied.

He shut the door behind him.

What a farce. In the space of twenty-four hours, I'd met two sacrificial beasts, a male and a female.

But why had Fei Fei come looking for me? Why…

The thought passed from my mind, and I went back to bed, only to be woken again when my professor phoned.

———

He said, 'Stop spending time with Charley, he's a dangerous character.'

'All he did was take in two sacrificial beasts,' I muttered.

He inhaled sharply. 'You've seen them?'

'Yes, one male and one female.'

'Stay away from them.'

'It's not like they eat people,' I pouted.

Anger lurked beneath the surface of his voice. 'At least stay away from the female.'

'Why?'

'Haven't you noticed? All the dead ones were males. Have you seen their tongues?'

'What do you mean?' I yelled, suddenly furious.

'You already know,' he said calmly, and hung up.

I stood with the phone in my hand, shaking all over. I thought of that kiss. The icy-cold forked tongue. I called my niece, but it was my cousin who answered. 'I want to speak to Lucia,' I said.

My cousin said she wasn't in, she was visiting the sacrificial beasts. 'The first group is being killed tomorrow, all the kids have gone to say goodbye.'

'They're really doing it?' I was astonished. 'How could they?'

'The higher-ups decided. A big delegation showed up – all the families bereaved by the suicides – howling and screaming that the sacrificial beasts must die. No point trying to protect them, anyway, they're just going to kill each other.'

'How will they do it?'

'Bullet to the brain ought to do the trick, no matter how strong their life force. But just to be sure, they'll get a lethal injection too. Belt and braces.'

As I listened to this calm recitation, my eyes grew wet. I was trembling violently all over.

—

Red River Square, in front of Cloudtop Towers, was full of people. I struggled through the crowd until I saw Lucia, sitting vigil with about twenty other kids silently holding up placards that read, 'Let the sacrificial beasts live.' Everyone else treated the protesters like lepers, glaring at them in disdain, and turning away.

No one cared.

Yong'an City was full of beasts. If one species died out, there'd be others to take its place, not to mention all the hybrids. *We treated you well to start with, but look how that ended up. This is all your own fault – you only have yourselves to blame.*

I hurried over to her. 'Lucia, Lucia, why aren't you going up?'

The little girl turned her tear-stained face to me. 'They won't let me, Auntie, but I know the beasts truly don't want to die.'

In a rage, I phoned my professor. 'I need to bring the children up. You've already decided to slaughter the beasts tomorrow, why not let them say goodbye? Make this happen, or forget about ever seeing me again.'

He could tell how angry I was. After a moment's silence, he said, 'Fine.'

A short while later, a man in uniform walked over

from Cloudtop Towers. Kind-faced, but I knew his heart was cold. As respectful as if he were meeting the queen, he said, 'Please come this way.'

Lucia and her friends looked at me with admiration, as if I were Batman or something. They followed me into the building.

—

I'd never seen so many sacrificial beasts in one place. In their individual glass cubicles, they were tall and well-built, every single one of them beautiful. Their eyes were clear and wise, but they looked at us with absolutely blankness. I shivered. These expressions belonged in a high-ceilinged temple, above a lotus blossom – on the face of Buddha.

None of you know anything. I thought of Fei Fei. How we'd embraced that night as I babbled at him like a child. He'd smiled and stroked my back. He knew, and I did not. I couldn't see through the fog, couldn't find my way out.

They looked at us like that, their bodies covered in scars, sometimes half their faces destroyed, but even so, they looked at us with those baby blue eyes, with the innocence of children. All of a sudden, I felt I had nowhere to hide. Flames flickered in my heart as shame turned into rage.

Just like that, I felt a strong sense that the sacrificial beasts might be the most beloved of the spirit world, the most perfect specimens of all creation. Us humans, and all other beings, were inferior products, rubbish tossed aside by the gods. This was a stab in the heart, such sharp pain I thought I might vomit.

Luckily, Lucia tugged my arm and said, 'Auntie, what's wrong? You don't look well. Are you sad?'

I turned around and looked at the children, but now they seemed like sacrificial beasts – young ones – staring back at me with innocent sympathy.

I burst into tears. I couldn't control myself, just bent over and howled.

A man in uniform came over and gave me a glass of water, patted me on the shoulder, and walked away.

Lucia led me to her favourite beast, a female. She looked a little like Ru Ru, sitting quietly in her cell, reading a book. Lucia rapped on the glass, and the beast smiled at her. There were little holes in the barrier, so we could hear her voice clearly.

'Lucia, are you here to see me?'

Lucia's little face was etched with worry. She asked in a small voice, 'Ching Ching, are you going to die?'

'Yes,' said Ching Ching, 'We all are, but it doesn't matter. It doesn't matter in the least.'

Lucia was trying not to cry, and Ching Ching

comforted her. 'Maybe we won't die. One of us will survive, or maybe a couple. You can come visit us then, Lucia. Bring us lemon soda and bananas, our favourite food.'

'All right,' said Lucia.

Ching Ching reached out as if to touch her, but the glass was in the way. Her arm was slender, the skin thickly marked with cuts, deep ones, like plough lines in a field. It was a horrifying sight, but still, she was alive.

I left Lucia slumped by the glass, whispering to the beast. Her little face was full of sorrow, her eyes glittering with tears.

The next few cells all held males, even more heavily scarred, one of them missing an arm, but all still alive. They sat there, or swept the floor, or ironed their clothes – they would all be dead the next day. I could barely contain myself, they were so calm. None of them showed the slightest sign of violence, and it was easy to forget how vigorously they'd once tried to damage themselves. In the last cell was a male beast whose entire face had been eaten away, as if by strong acid. His eyes were still beautiful. He held a small knife and, as if sharpening a pencil, was cutting slices off his fingers, long slivers of flesh falling to the ground. His ruined face split open in a smile. Blood trickled down it.

I'd been holding it in, but now I was violently sick. When I'd finished vomiting, I turned around and fled.

—

My professor phoned while I was heading down in the lift − it was impressive that they had reception here. He said, 'Zhong Liang's waiting for you downstairs, look out for him.'

'Who's Zhong Liang?'

At the ground floor, I found the student I'd met a few times before, though I'd never asked him his name. So this was Zhong Liang, my professor's latest lapdog. Beaming, he walked over and said it was good to meet an alumna.

'Don't call me that,' I said, 'I never graduated.'

He kept grinning. A young, handsome man − even his fake smile was dazzling. He said, 'The prof always says of all his students, he's proudest of you.'

I couldn't be bothered trading jabs with him, and turned away. I knew my face was pale.

Zhong Liang grabbed my arm to stop me leaving. 'Let's go get a cup of coffee, and I'll tell you the story of the sacrificial beasts.'

—

Zhong Liang sat opposite me, sipping his latte, looking every inch like the pampered, rich kid he was. When he spoke, he sounded exactly like our professor. 'The sacrificial beasts were originally one of the big clans. They dwelled in the mountaintops, and hardly owned anything, living in poverty. There were more males than females, a typical matriarchal society—'

'Skip the official version and get to the point. Why are so many of them dying?'

'They were killed,' he said simply.

He doesn't want to die, Lucia had said.

'The female beasts have all the power. The males don't speak because their tongues are slit at birth, and then they get slaughtered. Lower numbers mean better treatment for them. As an endangered species, they're entitled to protection. Now they live well. No one hunts them, and they don't need to work. To maintain the status quo, a male beast is sacrificed every month. Newborn females are killed, males have their tongues slit – and they live a long time, so the female beasts can go on the way they are—'

Before he could finish, I'd abruptly stood up and started dragging him out. He said, 'What are you doing?'

'Stop talking, we're going to see that bitch.'

—

Overpowering the female beast Ru Ru was very simple. Zhong Liang and I tracked her down at the Dolphin Bar. She was sitting there alone, drinking with a melancholy expression on her face, while Charley was nowhere to be seen. Zhong Liang walked over, took the bar stool next to hers, and stuck a hypodermic needle into her. Easy as pie – no wonder he was my professor's favourite student. Ru Ru crashed heavily to the ground.

Zhong Liang let out a breath and said, 'Sacrificial beasts are very strong. This is seven times the regular dose.'

'Seven times?' I frowned, and did a quick calculation. That would have knocked out ten elephants.

He slung Ru Ru over his shoulder, which caused a stir. The bartender came over and asked me, 'What's going on?'

Zhong Liang flashed his ID, slick as a security agent. 'This is an escaped sacrificial beast,' he said. 'I'm taking her in.'

He pulled back Ru Ru's hair to expose her long earlobe with its jagged edge.

The crowd quietened, and went back to their drinks. Just young people out for a good time.

—

I said goodbye to Zhong Liang and got a taxi home. On the way, I phoned my professor. He said, 'Are you planning to come back to the university?'

'Of course not,' I said.

'But you know,' he murmured, 'I've been waiting for you to come back.' With that, he hung up.

What insanity was this? Just as I was puzzling this out, Charley called.

And here was the insanity. Charley was in a fury, screeching into the phone, 'They took Ru Ru away!'

'Yes, didn't you know? This was a plot.'

Before I could explain further, Charley – normally such a gentleman – was roaring, 'What the fuck are you talking about, you stupid woman, why can't you think before you act, you'll get us all killed if you go on like this.'

I almost wept to be yelled at like that.

I was still at university when I first met Charley. I'd bump into him in the zoology department. He was neither a student nor a teacher, just a weirdo who always sat in the back row of the lab, looking like he wanted to laugh as he watched me carrying out my experiments. When I dissected an animal, he came over to criticise my scalpel skills. 'Girls shouldn't hold a knife like that,' he'd say, 'you're not chopping vegetables, you're not going to produce a tasty dish from this.'

He was tall and broad-shouldered, with regular features and long hair. His baggy clothes made him look like a rock 'n' roller, and in the sunlight, his skin was the healthy colour of wheat. I knew nothing about him, but his peculiar accent told me he came from far away. We became friends and saw each other at the lab every day. He often sat behind me. Strangely, my professor never tried to put an end to his odd behaviour.

'You shouldn't be doing this,' Charley would say, 'Find a good man to marry instead.'

I'd just laugh.

'You're cute when you laugh, you're actually a nice girl, but you're too sensitive, you get hurt too easily.'

That was a bullseye.

When I dropped out of school and drowned my sorrows at the Dolphin Bar, he kept me company. 'Get as drunk as you like,' he said. 'I'll make sure you get home safely, all right?'

And now he was screaming, 'You stupid pig, you moron!' Then he hung up.

I froze for a moment, then gave the driver a different address.

Charley's place.

—

My heart beat wildly all the way there. I kept trying to call Charley back, but couldn't get through. I tried my professor, but that didn't work either. It felt as if everyone in the world had vanished into thin air, until Lucia phoned sobbing. 'Auntie, did you hear? They killed the sacrificial beasts. All of them, every single one! Even Ching Ching!'

I stopped breathing for a second, and then I could only say, 'How could they, how could they, weren't they only going to kill the males?' Yes, I remembered my professor's words very clearly, just the males. But if he knew this whole thing was a plot devised by the female beasts, someone as devious as him would never start with the males.

Sure enough, when I got to the flat, it was empty.

Charley was gone, Fei Fei was gone, and of course Ru Ru had already been captured.

I jumped back into the taxi and gave another address: my professor's lab.

The driver chuckled, 'Why so worried, miss, did you lose your boyfriend?'

If only my life were that simple.

—

I couldn't find anyone at the lab either. In a sudden frenzy, I started smashing the specimens to the ground, ripping up records, overturning benches. Finally, a security guard showed up and asked, 'Miss, what do you think you're doing?'

I howled my professor's name, tears running down my face. 'I need to see him! Tell him to show himself.'

Instead, it was Zhong Liang who appeared.

He handed me a phone.

'Hello,' said my professor through the receiver, 'I hear you've torn apart my lab again.' There was a hint of laughter in his voice.

'What did you do to them?' I said. 'You tricked me.'

'Didn't you know?' he said breezily. 'It was in the news today – all the sacrificial beasts are dead, and now they've broken free of the cycle of life and rebirth, they can ascend to paradise.'

I took a deep breath, and then another. I'd just been a pawn in all this, an idiotic pawn. 'What about Charley? Where is he? You have no right to lock him up.'

'Same thing,' said my professor.

Zhong Liang handed me a folder of documents from six years ago, back when I was still a zoology student at this university, back when I'd first become friends with Charley. And there he was, in a series of photos, before and after, a string of experiments turning him from beast to human. They sutured together his tongue, pumped him full of hormones to change his brain chemistry, altered his bodily functions, until he could live like a human being. But he was a beast. In the first picture his skin was dark, his eyes were blue and beautiful, and his earlobes hung low, with a sawtoothed edge.

Ching Ching, Ru Ru, Fei Fei. Charley. All beasts. I would never see them again.

Sacrificial beasts.

Sacrificing themselves for a greater cause.

—

I went home like a lost soul and slumped on the sofa, staring into space. My tears wouldn't stop flowing. I slapped myself hard, but it didn't do any good. Charley was right to scold me. I'd blundered in without thinking, I'd been an idiot, a moron.

The sacrificial beasts hadn't wanted to die. They'd been murdered. By humans.

But why?

I phoned my professor, but all I could do was yell, 'Why, why did you keep killing them? Why?'

My professor laughed. 'There were so many sacrificial beasts, how could we have killed them all?

They massacred each other, the females turning on the males, we just did the rest. I didn't exactly deceive you.'

'But you did deceive me,' I snapped.

'You're too stubborn,' he said. 'So preoccupied with right and wrong, who's smarter than whom, who wins in the end. If you're too clever, too focussed on the prize, you'll lose sight of the greater danger behind you.'

The doorbell rang.

I opened the door to find not a killer, but a delivery man with a parcel for me. The return address was Charley's.

I ripped it open as quick as I could, but it was nothing, just a book. Only printed text, not a single handwritten word.

A storybook. Myths.

It read: In ancient times, this world had gods in it, and these gods created mankind. They sprinkled the earth, and soon there were thousands of human beings. But there were too many people, and they were too foolish, too greedy, so they began warring and killing.

Human beings wanted gold, food, horses. They chased the gods up to the mountain peaks, and took over the fertile plains.

Mankind became intelligent and sly. Some learned to build houses, others to cure sickness, and still others to make weapons. There was nothing they couldn't do, they thought. Apart from humanity, everything else was just material, food, foes – and all could be destroyed.

—

The sacrificial beasts didn't want to die, but were killed. Their life force was strong, and still they died, murdered one by one. The clever, strong male beasts had their tongues slit at birth, leaving them mute. The singing, speaking females became their mates, and so the next generation came into being.

One by one, they were imprisoned. They'd long lost their primeval instincts, and over their long history, had come to believe they truly were beasts. Yet their clear, empty eyes, when they looked at you, made you want to weep. Their skin was criss-crossed with scars, like furrows on a piece of farmland, giving growth to a fertile civilisation.

This was their secret.

Yong'an holds countless secrets like this, only known by those in charge. We live our foolish lives in the shadow of Cloudtop Towers, beneath the high-level biology labs, taking part in academic conferences, protecting rare species, entertaining ourselves, indulging our senses.

—

I was spent.

Unable to eat, all I could think of was kissing the male beast, his forked tongue moving inside my mouth. I couldn't sleep. My body felt no longer my own, and sludge flowed through my veins.

I went to a therapist. He sat on the other side of the desk and stared at me through thick-rimmed glasses. 'You have to learn to relax,' he said, 'All of this is just in your mind. Really.'

I sat there sobbing, shaking all over. He began elegantly filing his nails. 'Your time's up.'

Later on, he arranged for some of his worst patients to visit an asylum. 'Go look at how those people live,' he said, 'and you'll understand how much better off you are.'

And so we went. Three hours on a bus, out of the city, to a small town. A river flowed past the willow trees, and beyond it was a white building. We stood on the second-floor balcony, looking down the airwell at the inmates.

They seemed peaceful: reading, drawing, or just staring into space. Some were murmuring quietly to each other, all even-tempered. Compared to them, we seemed like the ones who were crazy to have come all this way just to gape at them.

A doctor gave us a guided tour. This was a high-class place, designed to look like a holiday resort, all very well-appointed. Out the window was a coun-tryside scene: low clouds and a pale blue sky, like the most benevolent eye.

As we walked down a shady avenue on our way back to the bus, we passed by a group of inmates. They marched along in silence, not even glancing at us. One of them was Charley. Was it Charley? I wasn't sure, but I thought I saw him, just the way I saw him all those years ago: that irreverent expression, the long hair, a handsome man brushing past me.

It was him.

I wanted to believe that it was him, that my profes-sor hadn't killed him. I chose to believe what Ching Ching had said, 'One of us will survive.' *One god will stay alive.*

Back in Yong'an, I went to drown my sorrows at the Dolphin Bar.

The bartender said, 'Charley hasn't been in for a long time, all his girlfriends miss him.'

I burst out laughing. 'Are you telling me they can't find new boyfriends?'

He laughed too. 'Of course they will, even better ones.'

—

The sacrificial beasts were godly beasts. In ancient times, the males ruled the heavens and earth, and the females raised the next generation. Then they created humans, and humans tempted the females into slaughtering the males, slitting their tongues to leave them mute. They were driven into the mountains.

Their life force was strong, and so the tribe allowed the finest males to escape, to propagate the species. For thousands of years, these beasts were massacred but they never died out.

As for their extinction, no one can agree. Some say they were wiped out by humanity; others that there was an internal division, that the females wanted to eliminate the males, only for the humans to make use of them to carry out their own diabolical plan.

The sacrificial beasts were melancholy by nature, for they could see the true desolation of the mortal world. Their hearts were all-knowing, and could not be ruled.

Ultimately, the sacrificial beasts died out, and as a result, mankind inherited the world. They martyred themselves for us, hence their name, sacrificial.

IMPASSE BEASTS

The impasse beasts came from the east. They arrived during a period of unprecedented violence in Yong'an, when the city was under curfew, and soldiers were patrolling the streets with loaded firearms. The beasts showed up in lorries whose license plates had been worn through on the long journey, so no one could tell where they'd originally come from. Once they got to Yong'an, they were unable to leave, and so they settled here. When anyone asked, they said they were impasse beasts.

Impasse beasts are creatures of few words. They live in the west of the city, where there is a notorious reform school. The students are all orphans, and there's no wickedness they won't stoop to, not even robbery or murder. The impasse beasts are their teachers. Only a few years after the beasts arrived in Yong'an – before the elderly among them had time to die, before even the young had time to be born – the two lorries they'd arrived in were taken away by the authorities and placed in the museum of zoology. By that point, the unrest of the earlier period had been completely forgotten.

They are a tribe of unusually silent beasts. Their eyesight is poor, their appetites enormous, and they're constantly bullied by their pupils. Yet they seem to feel no pain, and never fight back. Everyone says how awful their lives must be.

The municipal government once invited them to a meeting, and asked their representatives to speak. Everyone hoped for a stirring narrative, but the beasts merely peered through their thick glasses, and lowered their heads to sip their tea, not uttering one word. Furious at this snub, the higher-ups declared that they were done, and the beasts could sink or swim on their own.

Impasse beasts are small in stature, with yellowish skin and a greenish tinge to their features, which are not beautiful. Their hair is very long, straggly from lack of nutrition. From a distance, they look as if their heads are sprouting weeds. Absolutely pathetic. Despite their poor eyesight, they read many books, and travel to many places, so when they do speak, they always have fascinating insights to offer.

Male beasts have fins between their toes, and their

fingernails are long and curved. The females have sharp noses with a white bone spur protruding from the tip. On sunny days, it gleams like silver. Their eyes are long and narrow, with thick lashes; they look as if they're crying even when they aren't. Other than this, they are exactly like humans.

There is much curiosity about the origin of their name. Some think it comes not from them being stuck in Yong'an, but rather from being descendants of a lunatic who lived in ancient times, a reference to the proverb 'crying at an impasse'. This is merely an urban legend, with no basis in fact, and, of course, can't be printed in even the least reputable academic journals.

People always mention impasse beasts in the same breath as chain gangs, farmhands, and prostitutes, as a sort of lowly, coarse labour. Not much research has been done about them. No one but an impoverished fiction writer who only ever publishes in literary journals would write a word about them, but even so she'd gloss over the beasts themselves in favour of their symbolic value.

The reform school is in the west of the city, past the third ring road, on a patch of land that's allegedly being developed but really remains countryside. Next to the campus is an evil-smelling canal that hasn't flowed in years. The locals set up a little shop nearby that sells almost-expired biscuits and pot noodles at astronomical prices. The beasts put away a fair amount of food, and their wages all go on these low-quality foods.

No one in Yong'an is willing to come to this place. Parents threaten little children, 'Do as you're told, or I'll send you to High School 72!' (The official name of the reform school.) Even the toughest kids are scared to tears. There is no public transport here; you have to walk twenty minutes along the tow path before you see the sign for the 767 bus, which only comes twice an hour, and often skips this stop. As a result, very few people ever lay eyes on an impasse beast.

—

All April, I drank alone at the Dolphin Bar. Every single night ended with me drunk and sprawled on the table asleep, or else quietly spewing my guts out in the toilet. Everyone in the bar knew who I was, but no one ever said a word to me. Only the bartender had the courage to ask, 'Where's Charley gone? Why isn't he with you?'

I smiled and went back to my drink.

For a whole month, a blank space ran where my newspaper column should have been. My phone stayed off, and I refused to see anyone. *Let me vanish from the world.* Only when it got dark enough for the trees to melt into the gloom would I return home, stumbling alone into the lift. Sometimes there'd be a few letters waiting for me, sometimes nothing at all. I'd sit by the window staring into the empty air all night, slipping into sleep at dawn. I never dreamed.

Sometimes I'd have brief spells of dizziness, or everything would go dark before my eyes. I'd get headaches, and suddenly start sweating from every pore. Once, I bumped into a long-standing acquaintance at the Dolphin Bar who exclaimed, 'My god, what happened to you?' But that was just in passing, we then nodded in greeting and moved on. Yong'an has too many wanderers, too many philosophers. Who has the time to care about anyone else? Who even remembers who other people are?

One night, as I was downing my eleventh drink, someone pulled out the chair across from me and sat down. 'Are you happy?' he asked.

He was in a white long-sleeved shirt, suit trousers, black leather shoes, and a tie, looking for all the world like a timid insurance salesman. I imagined the next thing he'd say would be, 'Want a joy policy? Only a thousand yuan a year, and after a decade, we'll give you ten yuan every time you're sad – after our firm has made a rigorous assessment of your mood, of course.'

But no, fortunately, all he said was, 'Are you happy?'
I looked up at his piteous face, scrawny behind thick
glasses, his long hair tied back in a ponytail. I slurred,
'Who are you?'

'I'm an impasse beast,' he said.

And that's how I came to know this beast.
Something like that. To be honest, by the time I'd
sobered up, my memory was a bit patchy.

———

The next time I remember seeing him was at home.
He was sitting in front of me, bent over a book. As I
came back to consciousness, my head felt like it was
splitting apart, my body hollowed out. Again, I asked,
'Who are you?'

'I'm an impasse beast,' he said, closing the book,
smiling. 'You've tamed me.'

I lost my mind.

The impasse beast was named Yue, and he was as
sombre as my grandad. I started screaming at him,
insisting that he leave my house at once, but he
remained calm and went into the kitchen, returning
with a dish of millet porridge. Next, some seasoned
cucumber strips, eggs scrambled with tomatoes, and
braised garlic aubergine. 'You must be hungry,' he said

to me. 'Go on, eat.'

I hadn't eaten a proper meal for half a month, and my defences were no match for this candy-coated bullet.

I sat across from Yue and gobbled down the food while he continued reading, looking up from time to time to smile like a benevolent dad. As I ate, I muttered, 'You'll have to leave after this meal. I'm used to living alone, and I don't need a tame beast.'

Unruffled, he read to the end of the page and closed the book, marking his place. Then he produced a wallet from his shirt pocket, at which I rolled my eyes. 'You think you can buy me with money?' I sneered, only to realise at a second glance that the wallet was mine. Yue laughed again, and said slowly, 'I found this in your pocket, when I was washing your clothes. Let me stay and you can have it back.'

Only then did I notice that my pigsty of a flat was now incredibly tidy and faintly scented with roses. The dirty clothes I'd usually fling all over the place were nowhere in sight, and my shoes were neatly lined up in pairs. 'You... you did all this?' I stammered.

'Yes,' he said. 'From now on, I'm living here. You can come and go as you please. I'll tidy your home, cook your meals, and do your laundry.'

Just like that, I'd domesticated him. Like having a

free houseboy, I told myself.

Maybe because I'd just eaten a nourishing meal, when I looked at the beast again, I found myself smiling. But then a thought occurred to me. 'Why did you want me to tame you?'

'Don't you write stories about beasts?' said Yue. 'I want you to write about us. No pressure. Whenever you have some free time, I'll tell you about impasse beasts. If you don't want to hear it, I'll stop. Write about it or not – it's up to you.'

He was respectably dressed, a little shorter than me, with the pinched look of an impoverished scholar from olden times, meticulous in everything, scrupulously proper at all times. I nodded. Truthfully, there was no way I could have refused.

—

I asked Yue, 'What did you do before?'

'Music teacher.'

'So you were at High School 72?'

'Yes.'

'Are the students there really so awful?'

'Not at all. They're good children, very well-behaved.' He smiled with infinite love, radiant as a saint.

I was touched.

'You have no idea,' said Yue. 'The students at our school might not be in a good place when they come to us, but by graduation, they've become proper members of society. As teachers, we educate everyone regardless of who they are, straightening out their minds and passing on knowledge. It's hard work. We might be beasts, but we still understand the importance of learning.'

I would have said they understood it better than most humans. I thought back to my professor, who'd lectured with such brio, he all but jabbed holes right through the blackboard. Once, an unfortunate classmate had raised his hand and asked, 'Sir, could you speak a little slower? I don't understand.'

He'd glared at the boy and said, 'Don't take this class if you can't keep up.'

Everyone burst into laughter, and the boy blushed bright red. He never showed up again.

Later, I'd told the professor, 'That was uncalled for – no need to be so mean.'

'How was that mean?' he said. 'If you don't understand what you're hearing, then stop listening. Do you really expect spoon-feeding? You aren't infants.'

That's why I was moved by what Yue said.

'Yue,' I said, 'I'm going to write a story about your kind, a good one.'

He smiled. 'There's no way of knowing whether it will be a good story or not. I'll tell it slowly, and you can listen.'

'Yes, all right.' My head bobbed up and down. He had utterly conquered me.

—

A week after I tamed the impasse beast, I was once again rosy-cheeked with health, and a semblance of order came back to my days. I spent much less time at the Dolphin Bar, preferring to stay at home reading or watching TV with Yue. Yet every night, I had the same nightmare featuring myself as a little girl, climbing a mountain – only the mountain was made of ash, with a gaping hole in the middle. The adult me could clearly see that the peak was about to collapse, but I was unable to shout a warning, and could only watch myself be buried alive.

I'd wake up in a cold sweat, sometimes screaming as well. Yue would come and say, 'What's wrong? Don't be scared, I'm here.'

There were fine wrinkles on his face. When he took my hand, even though his claws were as sharp as any ferocious beast's, I felt as safe as if he were my father.

I told him about Charley, sobbing. Yue said, 'It's

all right, things will get better. None of this really matters.'

These words magically put my heart at rest. I looked at him like he was a god, and said, 'Yes, I believe you.'

I threw my arms around him and stroked his hair, which was coarse and springy like seaweed, long and a little tangled. He wore it swept back, and it seemed to be growing at quite a rate.

Around that time, a critic I knew passed away. Not many people showed up at the funeral, and afterwards I went to the Dolphin Bar alone. Looking forlorn, Yue watched me leave and said, 'Don't stay out too late.'

I got to chatting with one of the bartenders. He said, 'It's good that he's not here – much quieter now. Not like Charley—' The other bartender gave him a vicious elbow jab, and he shut up.

I had to laugh. I'd only met the dead man a couple of times, but he had a bad reputation in our circle. He took drugs, smoked like a chimney, slept with every woman who came along, and some of the men too. He'd shout at people like a lunatic, and get into fights. If he hadn't been a critic, he'd have been hauled off to a labour reform camp long ago.

And now, he was dead. One less evil in the world.

The other bartender, the one who had elbowed the first, was very young. He sighed, 'It's always sad when someone dies. I used to hate this guy, but actually, the last few times he came in, his temper seemed to have improved. Now all I can think of is his good points.'

We laughed at the boy. He was so young – bright red lips and gleaming teeth, eyes as dark as ink.

The older bartender took a drag on his cigarette and said, 'He told me he was trying to change, but change what? You can't stop a dog eating shit. He wanted to stop smoking, stop drinking, stop taking drugs, and now look – he's dead!'

Another burst of merriment. Someone said, 'What an idiot. Smoking makes you immortal.'

Something choked me, and I started coughing. All of a sudden, this conversation felt horrible. I said, 'I'm leaving.'

They were still chuckling as I walked out. I walked down the pitch-dark street, thinking about the dead critic. I reached for my cigarettes and lit one. As I inhaled, my head swam as if I'd never smoked before.

I sat down on the edge of a planter. Yue phoned just then. 'Why aren't you home yet?' he said. 'I'm worried about you.'

For a moment, I couldn't speak. My mum used to

phone me if I was out late. 'Come back quickly,' she would say. 'I've made your favourite dinner. Come home.'

Come home?

But I had nowhere to call home.

—

Yue and I were sprawled on the balcony, sunbathing. He told me about the mass migration of the impasse beasts. When the tide of war swept over their homeland in the east, some were killed and others fled. They became wanderers, departing amid animal howls of anguish, moving in fits and starts, passing through the Gobi Desert across mountains and rivers, through the great plains and lakes, until they arrived at Yong'an.

'This is a good city, better than many others,' he said. 'We've had a good life here.'

That chilled my heart. The impasse beasts loved this city, but its residents treated them as a joke, as second-class citizens. They lived in the most impoverished district, in utter destitution, yet thought of this as a 'good life'.

'What does that mean, a good life?' I said teasingly.

Yue's eyes sparkled behind his thick glasses. 'Having enough to eat.'

It was all I could do not to shed tears.

My phone rang at that moment. It was my professor, whom I'd all but forgotten. Not even saying hello, he barked, 'Have you tamed an impasse beast?'

Are you going to dissect this one too? Out loud, I said, 'No.'

'Don't lie to me. Bring him here right now, and don't say anything to him.'

'Don't tell me what to do!' I snapped, suddenly losing my temper. 'You're a professor, a member of the elite, not a lower-class creature like us. Of course you're lording it over us, all high and mighty. But actually, you know nothing at all.' With that, I hung up.

Yue asked who the caller was, and I said it was someone I hated.

I'd known my professor for eight unlucky years. He was self-important, self-centred, self-serving, and downright selfish. I'd had enough of him!

When people in Yong'an talked about beasts, they told stories about meeting or spotting these creatures, slicing them up or analysing them, but no one ever wanted to know what kind of lives they led. This city had its share of suicides, and even more accidental deaths; plenty of happy people, but even more in despair. The impasse beasts had come from a faraway, impoverished place, and in Yong'an, they'd formed a community with the students at the reform school. They were small and ugly, and everyone made fun of them; yet they had found contentment.

Did the humans know how shameful this was?

I started writing the story of the impasse beasts by hand: how they began their migration in two large lorries, throwing dirt up as they sped along. They had voracious appetites – even now, Yue would finish any food I left behind, always apologising. 'I've already given you so much trouble – I hate to eat so much.' When I brought home cake, he always made me have the first slice, claiming not to like baked goods. The beasts were often hungry.

Yue said, 'One of us was so ravenous, he ate himself alive as we passed through yet another city. He started with his right hand, and then his left. It was a sudden madness, and no one could stop him. The people of the city just looked coldly on, no one tried to help.'

'Do you hate humans?' I asked.

'No,' he said, 'they have their own lives to lead.'

Even so, the people of that city got their comeuppance. A plague swept through, and people started killing themselves as if it were a competition, until there was nothing left but an abandoned ruin.

I told Yue about the plague, and he sighed. 'Such a shame. It used to be such a joyful place.'

I wrote all of this into my story. I had an impasse beast fall in love with a human woman in this city, only she wouldn't give him a single morsel of food, and so he devoured himself right in front of her, leaving nothing but his heart, which he presented to her.

I showed Yue the story and asked, 'Do you like it?'

He smiled like someone from a previous generation. 'You're a real storyteller.'

Storytellers are irresponsible. All we do is make things up from existing events. As for the actual stuff of life, we know absolutely nothing about it.

I was aware of this.

Many years ago, I had fled the science lab and become a writer. For a long time, I wrote romances. My professor phoned to yell at me. 'Everything you come up with has been written five hundred times before. I just have to look at the beginning of any of your stories, and I know how it ends. You make me want to vomit.' Even so, my novels had sold extremely well, and I soon earned enough money to buy a flat, and my royalties were sufficient to live on.

Finally, the day came when even I found this unbearable, and so I switched to writing stories about beasts. No one wanted to read these, but my food and drink column in the local newspaper was a success. My editor kept urging me to seek out more delicious things. 'Keep this up,' he would say, 'and I'll give you a raise next month.'

Nobody knew about the beasts. Their stories were all sad.

—

I was thriving. Back when I was alone, things were never this good. I asked Yue, 'Will you leave when I've finished writing my story?' My face was probably alight with hope.

He smiled. 'Of course I'll leave. You haven't been to High School 72. The children there have no parents, no one to love them. They want me to go back. I'll teach them to sing, and you can come visit. The 767 will take you there. I'll come on my bike to meet you at the bus stop. The whole school will be singing at a concert on Monday. We sound good. The locals from all around will come and see us.' He sounded proud, playing with his hair which fell over his chest, all the way to his belly. I said, 'Your hair's got longer.' He said, 'Yes, I've been eating so well here, my hair's grown fast.'

He was an excellent cook, and even his ironing skills were superb. A little sadly, I said, 'How will I manage, when you leave?'

He smiled and said, 'You sound like my little daughter.'

His little daughter had died back in his home town, that distant village in the east. He told me she was very beautiful, just a little beast but already the bone at the tip of her nose sparkled. Then he sighed.

'Are you happy?' he asked.

'Yes,' I said.

But the nightmares kept coming. I found myself dying in all kinds of ways, my younger self putting her neck through a noose or slicing off her own lips. Sometimes I dreamt of my mother telling me stories of beasts. She said, 'These stories are all real, but you'll forget as soon as you've heard them.' I also dreamt of the first class with my professor, how he kept calling on me. His questions were all about stories my mother had told me, so I was able to answer them. His face lit up, and he proclaimed, 'You're the brightest student I've ever taught.' The next moment, though, he was cursing me, 'You're completely useless. Whenever I look at one of your novels, it makes me want to vomit.' I cried and laughed at the same time, startling myself awake.

I'd never been so well-nourished, with all the delicious food Yue was making, but I'd also never felt so hungry. Often, my insides seemed completely hollow. When I woke up crying in the night, he came to me and said, 'Don't worry, this will pass. You'll have a happy life.'

But I was afraid. I didn't know what happiness was. For many years now, I hadn't felt anything like joy.

I drank, but didn't get drunk. Cigarettes made me want to throw up. Chatting with Yue on the balcony, he offered me a snack every few minutes. 'Have some more,' he'd say. He ate a lot, and so I did too.

But still, I felt hollow and afraid. For some reason, the nightmares wouldn't cease.

—

My professor called me again. 'Do you still have your impasse beast?'

'I've never had one. Don't be crazy. And don't bother me. I'm doing very well, better than I've ever been. I'm so happy, there's nothing at all about my life that I would change. I'm healthy now. Stay far away from me.'

He was silent for a while. 'Who made you unhappy? Was it me?'

'Why ask, when you know the answer?'

One of us hung up, but I don't know if it was him or me.

—

The impasse beast story was almost done. Yue made more and more things for me to eat. Sometimes I'd run a thick wooden comb through his hair. The long strands flowed through it, never snapping. I said, 'You have such good hair.'

He smiled at me. 'What's good about it? Sorrow is as long as hair.'

'Aren't you happy?'

'I am, but other people aren't.'

'So it's the state of the world that's making you sad?'

He was silent for a moment. 'Are you happy?'

'I'm happy,' I said. 'Truly.'

'Good,' he said.

—

That evening, I suddenly decided to pay the Dolphin Bar a visit – not that I particularly needed a drink, but I missed my old friends. I said to Yue, 'I'm going down to the bar.'

'All right,' he said. 'Don't stay out too late.'

'I won't be long,' I said. 'Just a quick one. I'll be back before midnight.'

He reached out and tousled my hair. His finger-nails were sharp and very hard, and my scalp tingled as they scraped across. I looked at his face – weak, a little prim – and felt a chill rise from my feet. My mother told me long ago that beasts are beasts, and that no matter what, will always be different from humans.

I was still thinking about this at the Dolphin Bar. My mind clung to his hands, or rather, his beastly claws, and those bone spurs on his ankles. I'd noticed that he'd scratched one of my sofa cushions to shreds. Of course, I didn't mind.

But I'd tamed him. My impasse beast.

Blearily, I heard the man next to me talking about the dead critic. Someone else said, 'Who knows how that guy died. He phoned me a while back, sounded over the moon. Said he'd tamed a beast. Then a while later he was sobbing. His beast went away.'

'Too many drugs,' someone else snarled. 'It was all in his head. I'd like to see him bring a beast in. We've got an expert here!' He elbowed me. 'There's a species called the impasse beast, right?'

'Yes,' I said. 'I've got one too.'

As soon as the words left my mouth, I thought frantically, oh no, oh no, this is why I shouldn't drink.

'Huh?' The man looked startled. 'You too? What's yours called? This guy said his was Yue.'

I stiffened. One week after taming Yue, the critic had died.

I hurried home and went up in the lift. I rang my bell, hands trembling. No answer.

It took me three attempts to get my key in the lock. I pushed the door open and called Yue's name. Nothing.

My beast was gone.

—

My heart was empty. He'd come when I was all alone, and now that he'd gone, I was all alone again. This wasn't right. I was empty. I could have walked into a wall. Instead, I slumped on the sofa, staring into space.

All alone, I laughed foolishly to myself. I didn't feel sadness or despair, as I'd expected, only joy. All alone, I laughed and laughed.

So many sweet memories. Me and Charley at the Dolphin Bar, the two of us matching a table of fifteen, shot for shot. Then there was the time we went camping in the countryside. He brought three girls with him, and their jealous sniping for his attention made me laugh and laugh. Though I was a girl too. My mum made me honey cake, but she was a terrible baker. It tasted disgusting, but I couldn't say so. So I learned how to flatter people. I did it to my professor. He said I was clever, so I showed him how clever he was. An 'A' on every test, and a place in the lab before I'd even graduated. He brought me to conferences and introduced me as his star pupil.

Then, suddenly, pain. Out of nowhere, violent and stabbing. I came to my senses and looked down, then dropped the knife in terror. When had I picked it up? My wrists were a cross-hatched mess. The blood flowed for a while before congealing.

I stared at it, feeling nothing but hilarity. This wasn't frightening, just funny. I phoned an acquaintance and said, 'I have a joke for you.' I giggled as I told her what had happened. She said, sounding stricken, 'What's wrong with you? Have you gone mad?'

I hung up.

The phone rang – my professor. 'Come to the lab right now!' he said.

'No,' I said. 'I'm fine where I am. Why should I go to that hateful place?'

He sounded more afraid than I'd ever heard him. His voice trembled. 'Come quickly! Unless you want to die.'

I was still laughing. 'So what if I die? I'm not scared. I'd be happy to die.'

He shrieked like a woman, 'Don't go anywhere! I'll send someone to fetch you!'

'Fine,' I chuckled. 'I'd like to see Zhong Liang,

why don't you send him?'

'Stop laughing,' he said. 'What's there to laugh at? Doesn't it make you sad that I'll never see you again? Don't you remember how you left? You won't come back. We won't see you. Doesn't that make you feel something?'

'No, why should it? I don't feel anything at all.'

I heard him sob, 'Why do you have to be so stubborn? I hate you so much. I wish I could kill you.'

That sent a pang through my heart. I felt weak. 'What are you saying?'

'I hate you. I wish you would just die.'

More pain. 'You're lying.'

His voice was rock-steady. 'It's true. The moment I first set eyes on you, I hated you. Everything I've ever done was intended to destroy you. I really, really detest you.'

I froze, and it took me a while to say, 'I'm very sad.'

'It doesn't matter how sad you are. I hate you.'

My mind seized up. I put down the phone.

A moment later, I started laughing again. As if nothing had happened. I went into the kitchen and heated up some leftover dumplings with instant seafood soup, whistling to myself, '*I'm just a lonely painter*'.

My eyes opened wide and I watched as my hands

reached into the boiling water to scoop the dumplings out, one by one. The water was hot, but that didn't matter. The dumplings were delicious. I was so content, so happy.

—

I woke up to see Zhong Liang sitting across from me in a checked shirt, reading my story.

A blast of pain. My hands were wrapped in bandages.

'What happened?' I said.

His head jerked up and he looked at me, confusion passing across his face. 'You're up,' he said.

'What happened to me?'

'You almost died. I gave you a shot. You should be better now.'

'Better?'

'Are you happy?'

'Happy?' I grinned. 'No.'

'That's good. You're well again.' He grinned too. 'The professor was scared to death. Apparently, you tamed an impasse beast.'

'How did you know?'

'The professor thought it was all his fault. It must have been the shock of what happened to Charley that made you like this.'

'What are you talking about?'

He waved the sheets of paper in his hands. 'I'm reading the story you wrote about them.'

'And you want to know what comes next?'

'It's a terrible story. You get all kinds of things wrong.'

My blood boiled. 'You don't know anything.'

'I don't know anything about stories, but I do understand data. You wrote that students do well at High School 72, but you don't seem to know that they all die. Suicide, car accidents, unknown medical conditions. They all die.'

'You're lying.'

'It's true. The official figures are very clear, I can show you.'

'So why doesn't the government do something about it?'

He smiled mysteriously. 'It's a funny thing, despair. Without it, we'd all die. But too much of it leads to chaos. And when you sink too far into despair, the impasse beast finds you.'

I stared at him. He got to his feet and put the manuscript on the pillow next to me. 'The love story was quite moving, though.'

I had nothing to say to that. Everyone loves those vulgar things.

I sat alone on the bed, looking at my story and thinking of Yue, as well as all the other impasse beasts. 'We've had a good life here,' he'd said. 'You're like my little daughter.'

I never saw him again, nor any other impasse beasts.

—

Impasse beasts are creatures of few words. They come from the east, and have enormous appetites. What they feed on is despair. Their hair absorbs despair, and grows longer. Their bodies expand too, and they reach maturity.

These beasts are nomads. They travel in lorries, seeking cities with abundant despair, and settle down when they find one. The humans whose despair they feast on grow euphoric, but empty too. Not knowing despair, they become vulnerable, and so die easily.

No one dares to kill an impasse beast, because the despair he's eaten in the course of his life will surge out all at once. If this were to happen, the city would be consumed by violence and destruction.

As an impasse beast ages, his hair grows even longer, finally spinning itself into a cocoon that completely envelopes him – at which point, he dies. Impasse beasts live long, and a death only takes place once every few centuries. Each time, a protracted war follows, leaving countless cities in ruins.

According to legend, impasse beasts are the descendants of the most despairing humans who ever lived, those whose despair reached such a pitch that they were unable to carry on. Weeping bitterly, they turned back, and gave themselves the name 'impasse'.

FLOURISHING BEASTS

All flourishing beasts are female. They reside in herds and are placid by nature. Being green-fingered, they have made their living as gardeners since ancient times, and are particularly skilled at raising rare species. A corruption of the word 'flower' gives rise to their name, 'flourishing'.

The flourishing beasts live in the south-eastern corner of Yong'an City, in the Temple of the Antiquities. There, they grow all manner of plants in the back courtyard, filling it with fragrance all year round. The temple's flourishing Buddha is especially potent for people seeking sons or mates, and so it receives a constant stream of incense offerings.

The flourishing beasts have delicate features that are etched perpetually with worry. They seldom speak. Their pale skin is marked with pale blue crescent moons, and they have six fingers on each hand, but otherwise they are no different from any human woman. Their markings grow more vivid with age, turning first dark blue, then black. After this comes death. When a flourishing beast's life ends, her tribe cuts her into eight pieces, which are planted into the ground, and then watered with yellow rice wine. A month later, a flourishing stem appears, flawlessly white, firm and lustrous as jade. After another month, this stem sprouts four limbs; then, another month later, a face. Now beast-shaped, the wood continues to soften. One more month, and the stem snaps off: a new flourishing beast is born.

A young beast does not speak any human languages. She feasts on pollen and continues imbibing rice wine. After six months, she's the size of a three-year-old, with the features of a young woman. At this point, her words flow freely, and she brims with intelligence.

It is hard for flourishing beasts to reproduce. Of every eight pieces that are planted, only one or two survive. Conditions need to be exactly right, and the saplings are particularly vulnerable during their embryonic stage, when human merchants are wont to chop them down for their high-quality wood, to be manufactured into small, exquisite household objects and sold at astronomical prices.

Decades ago, there was an episode of unrest in

Yong'an City that ended unpleasantly. After the government had restored order, strict new laws were introduced to prohibit this practice. But the profits were just too enticing, and flourishing wood continued to be chopped down.

Flourishing beasts are peaceful and benevolent by nature. They live on honey, rice wine, eggs, and cauliflower. They eat no meat at all, since they are born to take holy orders. When the women of Yong'an have nowhere else to go, they retreat to the Temple of the Antiquities. There, they tend to the plants, or take care of the sprouting beasts and cubs. All live in harmony, with everything they need at hand.

—

One day in March, Zhong Liang came to visit me with a large box of instant noodles. Chuckling, he set it down. 'A gift for you.'

I looked sidelong at it, annoyed. 'Zhong Liang, are you trying to murder your elders? There's got to be enough preservatives in here to turn me into a mummy.'

He laughed some more. 'All right, tell me what you like to eat, and I'll bring you that instead.'

'Forget it,' I said. 'What do you want?'

He scratched his head. 'There's a family gathering

at my uncle's house next week. I'd like you to come with me.'

'Why would you want me to come to a family gathering? Are you asking me to be your girlfriend?'

He looked as if he'd just stepped on a landmine. 'I wouldn't dare,' he said, which meant, *You're too old for me.*

'My uncle likes your stories,' he went on. 'When he found out we were friends, he told me to invite you.'

Ah, a fan. 'No way.' I never agreed to these kinds of requests.

The boy had a trick up his sleeve, though. He brought his handsome face close to mine and said, 'The professor might be there. Will you come?'

'Sure,' I blurted. Annoyed at having been so easily lured into revealing myself, I didn't say anything else, just shoved him out of my flat.

'I'll pick you up at six next Friday!' called Zhong Liang as I closed the door on him.

———

By the time Friday rolled around, I'd completely forgotten what I'd agreed to. I was lounging in front of the TV, eating ice cream in an oversized shirt, rumpled and unwashed. When Zhong Liang knocked on the door and I opened it, we looked at each other in shock. 'What the hell are you wearing?' we chorused.

He was all dressed up in a proper suit, standing very straight with a solemn expression. Were we going to a funeral?

I remembered then about the gathering and, without even stopping to apologise, rushed into my bedroom. Five minutes later I was back, having pulled on a pair of trousers and scraped my hair back into a ponytail. That was the best I could do. 'Let's go,' I said.

Zhong Liang stared at me with a strange expression for a full three seconds before his face twitched. 'Fine.'

—

Half an hour later, Zhong Liang's Fiat was pulling into the city's richest district, and I had an inkling that I was in trouble. He turned into the broad courtyard of his uncle's house, and I knew I'd been tricked.

That's how I ended up sitting across from the city's most famous jeweller, Zhong Ren. His nails were perfectly manicured as he took my hand, his grip firm and powerful. 'Hello,' he said.

I smiled foolishly. An empty smile. 'Hello,' I replied. Inwardly, I cursed Zhong Liang a thousand times. Why call this a *gathering*, when I was meeting his uncle one-to-one?

Like a fish laid out on a slab, I was there for my reader, Mr Zhong Ren, to examine. Zhong Liang sat in the window seat with a thick book in his hands, leaving us in the living room, facing each other like the two sides in a cold war negotiation.

'I like your stories,' Zhong Ren said.

'So kind of you.' All I could do was repeat the lines I'd used thousands of times before.

'I've read everything you've written about beasts,' he said. 'You make it all sound so real. The beasts are more human than the humans, and the humans are beastlier than the beasts.'

I sipped my tea and smiled blankly. 'It's not really so clear-cut.'

We fell silent.

The man across from me looked kindly, as if he were my big brother, and his features were a little like Zhong Liang's, though there was a sort of awkwardness to him which I would only have expected in a young person. He was staring straight at me, from my forehead to my chin, then back up.

I felt goosebumps rising all over my skin. Finally, I said, 'Mr Zhong, I should really—'

'Let's get married,' he said, as if startled from a dream.

He sounded sincere. I choked. The book fell from Zhong Liang's hand and thudded to the ground. *Damn you, so you were eavesdropping.* For some reason, that was the first thing to pop into my head.

—

It's not that difficult to avoid a person, but avoiding an overeager, weirdly obstinate rich guy is a little harder. I kept my head down for the next week, but Zhong Ren managed to track me down even somewhere as chaotic as the Dolphin Bar, his besotted face suddenly appearing before me and insisting, 'Just hear me out.' I lost all hope and wished that the glass in my hand contained not beer but arsenic.

I phoned Zhong Liang to shout at him, shaking all over, 'This is all your fault, you bastard. You're not getting away with this.'

Zhong Liang sounded stricken too. 'Listen, my uncle's always been strange, but I hadn't realised just how crazy he was. I didn't think a woman like you could catch his eye—'

I shrieked and hung up. Taking deep breaths, I told myself: *don't get into a fight with a child, it's not worth it, he doesn't know how to appreciate a more mature woman…*

I sat with the lights off, waiting for his call. With

Zhong Liang no doubt constantly broadcasting my location, there was no way he wouldn't know where I was. And yet, silence. All night long, the darkness pressed down on my head.

Finally, I couldn't stand it any longer. I picked up the phone and dialled.

'Hello?' Perfectly nonchalant.

I tried to speak, but my courage failed me and I hung up. Trying to pretend nothing had happened, I burst into tears.

My mother used to say: 'Never cry, or your tears will water your sorrow and it'll grow.'

Finally, I picked up the phone and called another number.

As soon as I said hello, Methuselah knew it was me.

'What's wrong?' she said. 'Are you unhappy?'

'Yes,' I said. 'I want to come and stay for a while.'

'Come,' said Methuselah.

—

'My mother once told me, "Don't bother Methuselah unless you're at the end of your tether. I've already given her enough trouble."'

'Don't be silly,' Methuselah now said. 'It's been ten years, and I still miss her a lot.'

She sat next to me sipping her tea. Her hair was loose, just washed. It looked beautifully soft and glossy in the sunlight. A soothing scent hung in the air. I recognised it right away, from all the time I'd spent here as a child with my mother: incense from the burners, plants in the back garden, various birds and insects, as well as the damp, woody fragrance of Methuselah herself.

As ever, there was suffering in her face. She was old now, and since the last time I'd seen her, the markings on her body had turned a deep blue, the skin so thin and translucent it looked for a moment as if it were wrapped around nothing at all. She gently placed her hand on mine. 'Don't worry, of course you can stay here. Shall we put you in your mother's old room?'

I nodded yes, and took a deep breath. My spirit settled as I clasped her hand. Her six fingers were ice-cold.

She was a flourishing beast, and this was the Temple of the Antiquities. Finally, my heart was at rest.

—

A young beast took me to the guest room in the back courtyard. Her neck was long and elegant, and her pale blue markings were like butterflies beneath her skin. 'You can call me Locust,' she said, smiling. She must have been around ten, which meant she looked like a twenty-year-old human. Her voice was delicate and crisp. I'd never seen her before.

She seemed shy, and scurried off after saying she'd come fetch me for dinner.

Nothing about the room had changed, apart from the TV set that now stood in a corner, and the enormous electric fan which was suspended from the ceiling.

I sat on the sofa and looked out the window. The rear courtyard was as verdant as ever. Flowers I didn't know the names of bloomed in all sorts of unimaginable colours. The only ones I could identify were plum blossoms, swathes of them in soft pink and white. My mother once said, 'I love gazing at these more than buying a real silk dress from Heavenly Beauty Mall.'

I smiled.

That night, Methuselah made me tofu stew. An unfamiliar aroma rose from it, instantly appetising. We had it with rice. The fluorescent lights in the great hall burned steadily, and the news was showing on the wall-mounted plasma TV. Methuselah pointed at a gaggle of beasts sitting to our left and explained that they were all born after I'd left. I turned to look and saw the young beast from earlier, Locust, smiling right back at me. She had a refined beauty, and her eyes felt familiar to me, dewy and attractive. Methuselah said, 'You've met already?'

'Yes.'

'She likes you.'

I smiled. 'I like her too.'

At the other end of the great hall, a group of human women sat at a round table, eating the meat dishes that had been laid out for them. They looked even more sorrowful than the flourishing beasts, whose faces were naturally etched with suffering. Their hair was dyed all sorts of peculiar hues. All of a sudden, one woman threw down her chopsticks, buried her face in her hands, and burst into loud sobs.

Methuselah shook her head. 'Times have changed. Everyone likes to cry these days.'

The newsreel ended, and Zhong Ren's face appeared on the screen. He said my name. 'Where are you? I can't find you. Please come back quickly, I need to talk to you.'

Methuselah grinned slyly at me. My appetite vanished.

That night, though, I slept soundly and dreamed of my mother, young but with pure white hair. Sitting in the window seat, she was listening to a staticky radio, quietly singing along.

Her voice was faint and turned into moans of

pain, as if ants were nibbling at her entrails. Each cry stabbed into my ears.

I woke to find the sun high in the sky. I was covered in sweat.

———

I opened the door and saw the flourishing beasts outside, all dressed in white, heads bowed beneath the gorgeous flowering plum tree. They were mumbling a chant.

The young beasts were standing at the back, holding hands. I thought I saw them trembling. From the far end, Locust turned and saw me. There were tears in her eyes, and somehow she looked like my mother.

Over lunch, I asked Methuselah what had happened, and she told me that a flourishing tree had been cut down.

An elderly beast had died that January and, as usual, had been planted in eight segments, three of which sprouted. One of these had just been chopped down and stolen.

Locust took me to see the two surviving saplings. They looked lonely beneath the flowering plum tree. We could only stare at them from a distance. A face, with markings, was faintly visible on each.

Their limbs were just coming in, plump and

stubby, like a baby's.

'Beautiful,' I sighed.

Locust turned to face me. She had an eye-catching crescent-moon mark right across her left cheek, and her expression was sorrowful. 'It's not,' she said.

I waited for her to say more, but there was no more. She was a beast. Instead of words, a low growl rumbled in her throat.

—

The flourishing beasts at the Temple of the Antiquities were split into two groups: the older ones looked after the holy site, while the younglings tended to the plants in the rear garden. Locust and I were in charge of the flowering plum. 'Each of us is assigned to a plant,' she explained, 'and mine is this tree.' Her eyes were full of love, and although she was just a young beast, there was something motherly about her as she watered, fertilised, and pruned. She stroked the bark tenderly and said, 'Look, there was an infestation when I was four. It left behind these scars, poor thing.'

'You must have been scolded for that,' I said. 'What kind of flourishing beast can't look after a tree?'

She laughed. 'It's not like that. Even with flourishing beasts taking care of them, trees will get attacked by insects, they'll rot away, they'll die. It's the law of nature. That's all we get in this life, and all we can hope for is that we leave behind some good seeds.'

I patted her head. 'So young, and already you sound like an old woman.' My mother used to say these words to me too.

I was a little girl then. She'd taken me to pray to the flourishing Buddha, and I'd looked up and realised the white jade he was carved from was actually beast wood, pale and flawless.

My mother said perhaps it was in remembrance of the beasts who'd been cut down for their wood. The murdered beasts.

Locust and I swept the courtyard together. When we were done, she said she wanted to watch TV – there was a new series she was crazy about. It happened to be one that Charley and I had laughed over. I sat with her, trying to be patient, waiting for the commercial break so I could relieve my eyes with breast enhancement ads instead of this rubbish.

Instead, it was Zhong Ren's face that appeared on the screen. His chin was covered in stubble, and he looked unwell. 'Where are you?' he said. 'Come back soon. I have so much to say to you. Please marry me.'

Locust thought this was a trailer for a new series and looked excited about it, while I tried not to vomit. How could a man who'd been such a success in the business world, with so much money in the bank, be such a blockhead? He was scouring the world for me, while the person I actually longed to see remained completely silent.

I sighed.

In the end, I couldn't stand it any longer and turned on my mobile for the first time in days. Right away, I was almost deafened by the chorus of notifications. Most of the messages were from Zhong Ren, each one using almost the same words. I couldn't delete them fast enough.

There were a few from Zhong Liang too. 'Where are you hiding? Please come back. My uncle is tearing our family apart.'

Just as I was thinking, *serves you right*, the phone rang. An unknown number.

I hesitated before answering.

'Hello?' Silence. 'Hello?' Call ended.

That must be him. He'd hung up as soon as he knew I was all right, no doubt so he could curse my ancestors eighteen generations back. I burst out laughing.

Let him curse me. How much longer would this go one for? Back in the lab, the slightest mistake in an experiment used to get me such a scolding I wouldn't be able to eat for three days. He'd scream at me if my assignments were imperfect, or if I got something wrong in an exam. When I dropped out of school, he'd stared at me with such hatred, I thought he'd have dug out my heart if he could.

I laughed again at the thought and shook my head.

—

Methuselah summoned me for afternoon tea. She'd dug out a photograph of herself with my mother to show me. She'd just been a young girl then, about the same age as me now. Flourishing beasts are so short-lived. Like grass, they begin withering almost as soon as they're born.

In the picture, she was smiling so broadly that her natural expression of suffering was all but invisible. She and my mother were holding hands, standing in the rear courtyard.

Now she was old and crinkled all over. I could hear her bones rubbing together when she walked. Her skin came off in flakes, and the markings beneath it were almost black, like tiny bottomless holes.

She said she had a surprise for me. She looked pained, like someone in the final stages of an illness.

It was an album, highly decorated, full of photographs of white furniture.

Each of these had been made from the wood of a

flourishing beast whose life had been cut short. Those whose limbs had just sprouted were still tough, and could be turned into tables. Those whose faces had started showing were softer, and could provide natural cushioning when made into armchairs. Others were cabinets, sliced into pliable, thin segments, or ornamentally carved. Regardless, each article was white as snow, without the slightest flaw.

'Aren't they beautiful?'

'Yes,' I said, and I meant it. The flourishing beasts were so beautiful that their corpses couldn't be allowed to remain whole.

Methuselah kept turning the pages, and there was admiration in her eyes. Such beauty.

Chairs, tables, cupboards, sculptures, doors, all sorts of objects. The most striking were the ones with faces, their eyes half-open. They looked like living things. Clean, classical lines or flowing, modern curves. 'Every murdered beast is in here,' said Methuselah.

She closed the album and dropped it on the table with a thud. It sat there, thick as an encyclopaedia.

'I've read your stories.' She took a sip of tea. 'You should write about us too.'

I had to choke back a sob. 'I will,' I said.

—

That night at dinner, I kept my head bent over my food, for fear of seeing Zhong Ren's face on the TV screen. He didn't show up, and Methuselah smiled at me as I let out a sigh of relief. Thank god he'd finally given up.

Locust noticed my expression and leaned towards me. 'What's wrong?'

'She's just happy,' said Methuselah. 'Now she can leave this awful place. She can go drinking and party-ing again.'

Locust stared at me. 'You're leaving?' Tears began rolling down her cheeks.

Methuselah pulled the young beast into her arms and soothed her, staring all the while at me, brows crinkled. 'So rude of her. After living alongside human women for too long, our children learn to cry too.'

I blushed and pasted a vacant smile on my face.

Methuselah patted Locust on the head. 'I don't blame you for not wanting her to go. Back when you were just a sapling, it was her mother who took care of you.' She stroked the young beast's face. 'You spent so much time together, you even look like her. She tended all of you so carefully. What a shame you were the only one who survived.'

I froze, my eyes fixed on the little beast. She stared

back at me, eyes glimmering with tears. My mother's face.

All of a sudden, a trail of cold sweat trickled down my spine.

—

I couldn't get to sleep that night. I sat by the window, gazing at the shadowy outlines of the greenery in the courtyard. In the distance, the glow of the city swept the sky like searchlights. The only thing I could see clearly was the flowering plum by the beds where the beast saplings grew. My mother had planted this tree with her own hands. Methuselah was there too, and she'd said, 'I'll take care of her for you.'

My mother had died in this temple, and the plum tree still stood tall.

Out of nowhere, I heard sobbing, and then an anguished howl, like an injured wild animal. My palms prickled with sweat.

Another scream.

This was no hallucination. They were coming thicker now, those cries and moans, like a chorus of chanted scripture, filling the air around me.

The loudest shrieks were coming from Methuselah's room.

I jumped out of bed and ran over there barefoot.

The flourishing beasts were huddled outside her door, all dressed in white, the blue markings on their skin glowing in the dark through their clothes. I heard Methuselah yowling in pain, her voice shredded.

I strode through the throng of beasts, who didn't seem to notice me. They knelt there, shaking all over, letting out a keening wail.

As soon as I saw her, I knew. Methuselah was dying.

She lay in bed, eyes sunken and hollow. Cry after cry came from her throat. Her body was covered in gleaming black markings, and her skin was completely pellucid, peeling away. Plump worms, about the size of my thumb, were wriggling from between the cracks. They were snow-white and perfectly smooth, crawling slowly over her chest and limbs.

Flourishing beasts stood around her, holding down her writhing body, tears pouring down their faces.

I took this all in, then ran out into the courtyard. I bent over and threw up.

——

I left the Temple of the Antiquities the next morning. Locust saw me to the door, her face pale as she walked behind me, as if nothing extraordinary had happened. We were silent as we passed through the rear courtyard to the great hall, and then out.

She hesitated, then reached to take my hand. 'Methuselah died yesterday.'

'I know,' I said. Her six-fingered hand was as cold as ice, and the blue markings on her wrist looked darker than I remembered.

Involuntarily, I recoiled as if from an electric shock and stepped through the door, brushing past a pious pilgrim. When I turned back, I saw the pure white flourishing Buddha, like a tree rising to the heavens.

Locust was smiling grimly at me. 'Goodbye,' she said.

I took a taxi home. The sun was bright on this late spring day, and I felt as if I were finally awakening from a nightmare.

That feeling lasted till I got to my front door, where Zhong Liang was crouched like a plainclothes detective, or really, more like a human trafficker. He had panda-like dark circles beneath his eyes, and he was sucking on a cigarette. The ground around him was littered with butts. I turned and ran as if I'd seen a ghost, but he was too fast for me. In a few seconds, he'd caught up and grabbed hold of me.

'Let me go,' I yelled. 'I need to sleep. Your uncle's finally leaving me alone, don't tell me you've gone mad too.'

'My uncle's dead,' he said.

His mouth was right by my ear, and I felt his hot breath on my icy cheek.

———

Zhong Liang dragged me along to the funeral. As befitted a famous jeweller, the room was as heavily ornamented as a palace, and streams of people came and went endlessly. I felt yellow and shrivelled like old celery. Zhong Liang made me stand in front of his uncle's black and white photograph. Zhong Ren looked like a successful man, the sort who goes around breezily setting the world straight. He was handsome, I realised, with a scholar's good looks. I bowed deeply to him three times.

Zhong Ren's sister received me with the hauteur of a queen. 'So you're the girl my little brother spent all that time chasing after.' She squinted at me, and I just stood there enduring her scrutiny. Finally, she sighed, 'It's a shame he never married...'

My scalp prickled. Was she trying to talk me into a ghost wedding? Fortunately, she said instead, 'My brother left you something. I'll send Zhong Liang to get it.' I rejoiced – how lucky that modern society had shaken off superstitions like forcing women to betroth themselves to dead men.

Zhong Liang brought me to claim Zhong Ren's bequest. I protested all the while that I barely knew the man, I wasn't family, I'd done nothing to deserve this, I couldn't just take a handout… But he said nothing, just strode ahead with a dark expression, while I lapsed into silence.

We arrived at Zhong Ren's house. Because the property was being sold, most of the furniture had already been moved out, and it looked much more spacious than when I'd last seen it. Zhong Liang asked me to take a seat in the living room while he went inside. He emerged with a large box. 'Take this,' he said.

The cardboard box was for a 29-inch colour TV, but I wasn't naïve enough to think Zhong Ren had left me a television set. 'What is it?' I stammered.

How the mighty had fallen − not long ago, this young man had smiled radiantly and addressed me with respect. And now, he might as well have been a zombie as he stared at me, face blank, and said, 'A chair.'

A chair.

He was enough of a gentleman not to make me carry the box home all by myself, but the second we got it through my front door, he vanished as if fleeing a plague house.

Finally, I could lounge on my comfortable sofa. The first thing I did was get some ice cream out from the freezer. Fortunately, it was still within the expiry date.

I stared at the cardboard TV box as I ate from the carton, but I couldn't be bothered to open it. Why had this bizarre man given me a chair, after forcing me to flee my own home? I'd rather he'd been more like his nephew, and left me a crate of instant noodles.

Why a chair?

A thought struck me and I put down the ice cream. The squat, square box cast a dark shadow.

What kind of chair?

I got a pair of scissors and cut the tape, shaking all over.

A snow-white chair.

It was classically designed, of a style fashionable over ten years ago, made of a softly yielding material. Even an idiot could have guessed it cost a fortune. An intricate carving decorated its back, in the middle of which was the faint impression of a woman's face, her eyes half-shut. Unsettlingly, she could have been my twin.

I stared at her. She seemed to sense me, and her eyes opened wide. She looked back at me, and smiled.

I shrieked as my legs gave way under me.

—

I drank a glass of hot milk, scalding my tongue. Finally, the sense of unreality faded, and I came back to myself. When I looked again, it was clear: this was a flourishing beast who'd been turned into a chair after her untimely death, one of the eight that my mother had tended. Like Methuselah said, they'd all ended up looking like her, though Locust was the only one to survive.

This one had died and become a cosy chair with pleasantly rounded edges. Zhong Ren had touched every inch of her. Ten years ago, he'd liked her at first sight, and so he'd acquired her. Every day, in his vast house, he stroked her and spoke to her, finally coming to love her.

I shut my eyes and touched the dead beast's face. I thought I could still feel the warmth of his hand.

When Zhong Ren asked me to marry him, I had darted away like a startled bird. Now he was dead, and I could finally cry about it.

My mother died long ago, but hell does not exist in Yong'an City, and so the souls of the deceased drift aimlessly across the land instead.

I wished I could believe that Methuselah's soul would meet my mother's beneath the flowering plum tree, while Zhong Ren's could take this beast's hand

and warm her six ice-cold fingers with his breath.

Night in the city is as bright as day. Light seeped in through the window, burnishing the chair.

My tears plopped onto the floor. I could hear them clearly in the silence.

I called my professor. 'Hello,' he said.

'I've come back.'

'Are you better?'

'Yes, much better.'

Silence. We were both stubborn, and so insignificant. A stand-off.

Finally, I said, 'I miss you very much.'

He seemed a bit alarmed by this, and it took him a long time to say, 'Yes, me too.'

——

I sat down to write the story of the flourishing beasts, imagining the narrator as one of them. 'I died before I was born,' I had her say. 'I was hacked into pieces and turned into a chair. My limbs were ripped apart, my entrails mutilated. One day, a man bought me for a lot of money. Because he wanted me. He placed me by his bed but couldn't bear to sit on me, so instead he gazed at me and talked, touching my face and kissing me. My heart was still tender.'

There was a plum tree in the park too, but its

blossoms had long since fallen. It was so hot. The ladies at the Dolphin Bar wore less and less, and the number of one-night stands went up.

I published my flourishing beasts story: a lingering love affair, a little girl weeping, worshippers praying at the Temple of the Antiquities.

I had to smile. Everyone was intoxicated, and life passed by like a wisp of smoke.

But nothing in life ever stays unchanged. One day, Zhong Liang came to find me at the Dolphin Bar.

'I shouldn't have blamed you,' he said. 'Everyone has their own fate. I know that now.'

I bought him a drink; he held his liquor well. I could have made a bad boy out of him – but then would I get in trouble with my professor?

We were plastered by the time I called him a taxi. He flung his arms around my neck and refused to let go. I peeled them off and pushed him into the car, and even then he stuck his head out to call after me, like an overgrown child, 'Please don't be angry with me, it's because my uncle died so horribly. His tongue was bitten clean off, so I—'

I was sober before he'd finished the sentence, and froze so suddenly that someone nearly walked straight into me.

Back home, I used what was left of my Dutch

courage to rip the chair apart. I picked up the backrest and broke the face right across my knee. Sure enough, there it was, a strip of red amidst the white: a human tongue. I tried to pull it out, but it was embedded so deep, as if the wood had absorbed it into itself. There was no way to retrieve it.

The beast had grown jealous. She'd sensed he had fallen in love with someone else, and so she bit off his tongue the next time they kissed. That's why she smiled when she saw me. I hadn't imagined it.

—

Two days later, I got a package from the Temple of the Antiquities, with a note that read, 'Methuselah said to give you this.' It was a wooden headrest, exquisitely carved with fluid lines, snow-white and ice-cold, yielding to the touch. An object of value. Right in the centre, a woman's face was barely visible, not one I recognised. Another suffering woman who'd once tended a sapling. Her eyes were hooded, but when they looked at me, I could see Methuselah in them.

I clutched the wooden block on my lap. The face smiled at me. Just a smile, no words.

—

Flourishing beasts are white as snow, and their wood

is strong yet springy, a sought-after commodity. However, the vast majority of saplings are infested with worms, and grow up to be diseased creatures, covered in the blue marks of the pests that devour them from within. When the markings turn black, they die.

When a beast passes, the worms exit her body, which is then cut into eight pieces: head, chest, belly, four limbs, heart. These are buried in the soil, in the hope of further life.

When a beast manages to avoid the predations of worms, the entire community rejoices and chops the plant down to make furniture. This is the true calling of flourishing beasts, and in this form they can live for thousands of years. Such beasts will never speak again, but they will live in comfort and ease, their hearts at rest.

As for the worm-ridden unfortunates who will never be whole, they must live as diseased beasts, spending their days eating vegetarian food and chanting scriptures, praying to the flourishing Buddha to be liberated from this sea of troubles as early as possible. They adore all wood, or even envy it.

Flourishing beasts are placid by nature and dislike movement. Like a wild meadow that withers and blooms, they enact the cycle of nature, rising like a phoenix from its ashes. Only a very few ever attain their true form.

And yet the flourishing beasts remain at peace, for this is not their plight alone, but the fate of every living thing.

THOUSAND LEAGUE BEASTS

The thousand league beasts have been extinct a long time. According to legend, they could see a thousand leagues away, as well as a thousand years into the future, hence their name. Their far-sightedness led to catastrophe, and so they were slaughtered by other tribes.

The thousand league beasts left behind neither artefacts nor documents, and are only briefly mentioned in the *Yong'an Ghost Stories* as having slim, straight-backed bodies, long black hair, narrow eyes with ochre pupils, pale lips, reddish skin, elongated necks, and a sharp bone spur at their heels. Otherwise they were no different from human beings.

A month ago, the remains of a thousand league beast were discovered by the archaeologist Cai Chong.

—

It didn't cheer me up to read in the morning paper

that a pile of beast bones had been discovered. I was eating breakfast at the time, and almost spat out a mouthful of milk. I looked more closely at the article, and realised this was a rare occasion: the skeleton of a thousand league beast, with its stretched-out neck, spiked heel, and long, slender body. Just like in the books. Cai Chong himself took up most of the next picture, wearing a baseball cap and cradling the bones of a young beast – like a farmer would his harvest. He looked delighted. The text went on to talk about the habits of the thousand league beasts, their mating rituals, the mystery of their extinction, even the news that a property developer was refurbishing the nearby (hastily renamed) Thousand League Mansions, the whole thing narrated at such length it occupied a full two-page spread.

Before I'd had time to read all of this in more detail, my editor called to say, 'Why don't you make your next story about thousand league beasts? They're a hot topic right now.'

Before I could protest, he went on, 'I'll double your usual fee.'

I accepted right away, with enthusiasm, 'It's nice to be appreciated by at least one person!'

He chuckled coldly, and recited a phone number for me. 'That's Cai Chong's mobile. Call and find out the latest. We've already been in touch with him, he says you can visit the site.'

I hung up and tapped the eleven digits into my phone while I still remembered them. I got through.

'Hello?' A young man's voice, rather charming.

Unconsciously, I cleared my throat. 'Is this Cai Chong?'

'I'm his assistant. Professor Cai set off for the field this morning.'

—

I hurried to the archaeological dig. The outer perimeter was marked with the sort of yellow tape you normally only see at murder scenes. Cai Chong's assistant Jiang Tan led me through a narrow gap. He was a short guy with such fine-boned features they were almost girlish. I kept my eyes shyly averted from his. As we walked, he said, 'Professor Cai's suffered all his life, and finally he's going to be rewarded.' He had an expressive voice, the sort that makes a listener tingle so she just blurts out some response then looks around distractedly.

The thousand league beasts lived in homes made of rammed earth, which had survived remarkably well, some houses were even complete with roofs. The excavation site was full of little pits, like open graves. By each pit was a display table, like something in a shopping mall, on which were laid out TV sets, radios, clocks, microwaves, and so on, older models but otherwise in good condition. As I walked on, I saw a double bed, and the skeleton of a beast laid out on it, half-assembled. From what I could see, it was a male.

Jiang Tan stopped and stared at the bones, clearly moved. 'He was only in his twenties when he died,' he said to me. 'He ought to have lived much longer.'

'How old are these remains?' I asked.

'Sixty-eight years!' said Jiang Tan with some pride. 'Definitely one of the oldest ever found in Yong'an.'

'I see,' I nodded. It was all I could do to show my admiration for a field of study I knew nothing about. 'Do you have any interesting stories from the dig?'

Jiang Tan hesitated, and reached out to stroke the beast's long neck bones. 'We haven't discovered anything new.'

He looked concerned. 'Are you all right?' I said.

'Professor Cai's gone quite a distance,' he said darkly. 'I'm not sure when he'll be back.'

He looked like he was about to cry. I patted him on the shoulder, 'Don't worry, I'm sure he'll be back soon.' Then, 'Why don't we go for a drink some other time, if you're free?'

'All right!' he said happily.

Humans could be so simple-minded, I thought to myself. Sometimes it's necessary to deceive them so they can survive.

—

They say that the simple-minded hold their liquor better, and the guileless Jiang Tan certainly proved to me it wasn't just good luck that had kept him unscathed so far. Three days later, at the Dolphin Bar, I drank so much I had to run to the bathroom to vomit, while he kept downing glass after glass, his expression unchanging. I sank into despair. All I wanted to do was leave, but he was like a little duckling who'd imprinted on me, fresh from his shell. 'Stay a little,' he said, tugging at my sleeve. 'Just have one more.'

The bartender smiled kindly at me. 'Yes, go on, have one more drink. I'll give you a discount.' His eyes said: *so, it's come to this.*

I felt my soul leave my body, and clung on to Jiang Tan, sobbing. 'Please, stop playing dumb. Just tell me what you know about the thousand league beasts. All their secrets. Everything they knew. I'll split my writing fee with you. I'm begging you – tell me!'

He took a mouthful of his drink and looked at me, his eyes as clear as a child's. 'I don't know anything.'.

I almost slid off my bar stool. My stomach flipped over, and I threw up again.

I'd never felt such despair, not since my mother died. I got out my phone, but before I could call a friend to come pick me up and take me home, it vibrated in my hand. I froze for a couple of seconds before realising this was no hallucination. I answered.

'So you're finally answering,' said Zhong Liang's voice. 'I need your help.'

Without waiting for him to finish, I wailed, 'Zhong Liang, come rescue me! I'm at the Dolphin Bar.'

By the time he showed up, I was passed out on the table. Jiang Tan's prattling about his complicated love life over the last decade had lulled me into sleep. Zhong Liang tapped my face, calling my name.

Later, he told me that when I came to, I'd hugged him and burst into tears, then begged him to take me to see our professor. I didn't believe him.

'I don't care if you believe me or not,' he said. 'That moron was so scared of you, he actually shut up for a minute. You were crying so hard, I thought you'd start an earthquake.'

Blushing with rage and shame, I shouted, 'I'm older than you, show some respect, little boy! That's no ordinary moron, he's the man who discovered the thousand league beast.'

Zhong Liang's face changed – he was, after all, our professor's pupil. Like a begging dog, he inched closer to me. 'What did you find out from him?'

'Nothing,' I said. 'He wouldn't tell me anything.'

Zhong Liang sighed. 'You've gotten old. If you were still young and beautiful...'

I flung a book at him. 'You have a go, then! You're young and beautiful, offer yourself up on a plate and see if he bites!'

'Fine,' said Zhong Liang, not turning a hair. 'I'll give him a call.'

He called Jiang Tan's number. Call declined. He tried again. Phone turned off.

I looked sidelong at him and sneered, 'So you thought you could teach me a lesson, but it's Jiang Tan who is the true master.'

Zhong Liang let out a yelp as if he'd just remembered something, and his face turned pale. 'You have to help me: could you buy garlic scapes?'

For the second time that day, I almost fell out of my chair.

'You don't understand,' he whined. 'The professor lost his marbles yesterday. He told me I had to go find you and make you buy him scapes, otherwise he'd drop me from all his classes.'

It took me three seconds to understand this babble of words. My face twitched. 'Have you both gone insane? It's autumn! Where am I supposed to find garlic scapes?'

Zhong Liang grinned slyly, and pulled a supermarket coupon from his pocket. 'Four Seasons brand tinned scapes – two for the price of one!'

—

In the end, it was easiest just to go along with it. I followed Zhong Liang to Joyful Supermarket, which was absolutely packed. I jostled through the crowds, quietly cursing Zhong Liang, who'd disappeared to god knows where, while I was still reeling from my hangover, and looking everywhere for these mythical tinned scapes. Suddenly, there was a stabbing pain in my ankle. I spun round, and there was Jiang Tan, clutching a bag of frozen pig entrails, searching for something on the vegetable racks. I shouted his name and grabbed his arm.

He jumped in fright, and the entrails clattered to the ground. He stared at me for a second before breaking into a smile. 'Oh, hello. What are you buying?'

'Garlic scapes,' I muttered.

'Garlic scapes...' he repeated, an enchanting

sadness on his face. I was almost moved, but my novelist's instincts asserted themselves, and I forced myself to stay calm. 'When did you go to the dig today?' I asked.

'About six,' he said, as if it were nothing at all.

'So late?'

'No point going too early if there's nothing new to find. I thought I'd have a bite to eat first.'

'Give me a call if you think of anything interesting,' I badgered him.

'All right,' he said, reaching out like a kungfu warrior to grab a pumpkin, then picking the intestines off the floor. As he started walking away, he thought of something, and turned back. 'Tinned scapes are on the second shelf to your left.'

I looked, and there they were, Four Seasons brand, taking up half the shelf. Exactly like the TV ads. I grabbed one and went to pay, and there was little Zhong Liang, two people ahead of me in the queue, with so many snacks he might have been stockpiling for a famine. I tossed the tins into his trolley, and decided I'd done everything that could be asked of me.

And still Zhong Liang wouldn't let me off. 'Could you give the professor a call?' he said playfully. 'Tell him you bought the scapes, otherwise he'll scold me.'

Why not accompany the Buddha right up into the heavens? I listlessly took out my phone and made the call. He picked up on the first ring. 'Did you buy me a scape?'

'Yes,' I said, wondering if I was going to start laughing or crying.

'That's it?' He seemed unhappy.

'Yes.' I couldn't summon the energy to say any more.

'You'll have to do it again tomorrow.'

I thought I'd misheard him. 'What?'

'You'll have to buy me a scape again tomorrow.' His voice was unwavering.

'Like hell I will!' I hung up and stormed off, ignoring Zhong Liang as he wailed for me to come back.

For god's sake. I might be a nobody, but I had a living to earn. Everything cost so much. Did he think I was just sitting around waiting for him to give me a task?

I decided to phone Jiang Tan and pester him till he brought me to the site. If I could sniff out a few salient details, I might have enough for a short story that would pay in money if not tears. Alas, once again, he'd turned his phone off. The nerve.

—

Jiang Tan showed up that night – on my TV screen. Our local station was doing a special report on a female thousand league beast whose bones had been laid out on a slab. Jiang Tan stood nearby, pretty as ever. The camera panned across the huddled skeleton of the young beast, shreds of clothing clinging to the bones. 'We found her just this afternoon,' said Jiang Tan. 'Very well-preserved. Death by suicide.'

'Why did she kill herself?' the reporter asked.

Jiang Tan's smile could have brought down cities. Half of Yong'an held its breath. 'Maybe she was advanced for her age, and had early-onset depression.' I almost smashed my screen in.

In the middle of the night, the idea for a story came to me. If thousand league beasts knew everything that would happen in the next thousand years, then they'd be born knowing their own fate. Perhaps an entire generation of young beasts killed themselves exactly because of that, thereby ending their species.

Through that, I threaded a love story between two beasts. The ironclad rule of a newspaper fiction writer: never leave out the romance. The plot was full of holes, of course, but nobody expects short stories to make sense.

I hastily handed in my draft the next day. The love story was so mawkish, it was accepted right away. 'You wrung every bit of emotion out of the older beast falling for the younger,' my editor gushed. 'When the young beast committed suicide and the older one starved to death, tears came to my eyes.'

I laughed and hung up. Hugging myself, I sat on the balcony and enjoyed the waning autumn sun. When my professor read this shitty short story, he'd probably feel physical pain. The thought warmed me. I couldn't stop smiling.

When I first met him, I was a shy, awkward girl who didn't talk to strangers. I'd insisted on gaining admittance to the zoology department because I wanted to learn all about beasts. On the first day of school, he showed up in a black jumper, dark-rimmed glasses on the high bridge of his nose. He strode up to the lectern and stared at us for a beat, chewing gum. 'Forget everything you know,' he said. 'I'm here to rescue you.'

The lecture theatre burst out laughing, and I couldn't help joining in. I was third on the list when he took attendance. He called my name three times, pretending he couldn't hear because my voice was too soft. Irritated, I walked out, and he called after me in a rage, 'If you have the guts, don't ever come back!'

I didn't have the guts, so I came back. I wanted to study zoology, and he was the very best teacher we had, world-famous, a credit to our city and our school.

The last time we quarrelled, we actually ended up hitting each other. Pushed beyond endurance, he held me and roared, 'When will you learn to do as I say?'

'Never!' I spat.

He shoved me away with another roar and sat down. 'Where did you come from, to make my life this hard? Where did you come from?'

I stood firm, then finally I walked over slowly and sat down in front of him, crying.

He reached out to brush the tears off my face, looking upset. 'I'm sorry, don't cry. I know, I know.'

I stared at him. There were wrinkles around his forehead, and threads of red in his eyes. His features were etched into his face, and his lips were thin but strong. 'Stop crying,' he said.

That was the last time I saw him.

—

He tried to visit. The doorman, Fei, said, 'A middle-aged guy came looking for you, but you were out. He left this.' It was an envelope with my professor's handwriting on it, containing a copy of the newspaper with my story, and next to it an advertisement – 'Live in Thousand League Mansions, Enjoy a Thousand

Year View'. So that's why my editor wanted the story: to be part of someone else's sales pitch. I wondered how much he'd been paid for that. Across the headline, scrawled like he was marking an essay: 'This is dogshit.' I smiled grimly, then noticed he'd written below with a ballpoint pen, 'A SCAPE.'

Had he actually gone mad from craving garlic scapes? As far as I could remember, he had no strong passions except for mashed potato and beasts. I'd never seen him so enthusiastic. I pursed my lips, but didn't follow my instincts to toss the paper away. Instead, I thanked Fei and went upstairs to my flat.

I'd just come from the archaeological dig, where there'd been no sign of Jiang Tan, and Cai Chong wasn't back yet either. The only new item they'd found was a refrigerator, but it hadn't been opened yet – the team was still chipping away at the rust sealing it shut.

I opened my own fridge and got out the milk, then slumped on the sofa drinking from the carton. If my professor knew I'd been back to the site, he'd surely have been moved. *There's hope for you yet*, I could hear him saying.

No sooner had I had that thought when the phone rang. It was Zhong Liang. 'Your story about the thousand league beasts sucked.'

I couldn't be bothered getting angry. 'That's why you called? Did you lose your funding or something?'

'Not at all,' he said smugly. 'In fact, we're about to launch a new project. Guess who our professor met recently? You won't believe this, but it was Cai Chong! We're going to research thousand league beasts. He hasn't confirmed this, but I'm pretty certain.'

I felt something thud in my head. 'Cai Chong? The archaeologist?'

'That's the one.'

'When did they meet?'

'Maybe two weeks ago?' I counted on my fingers – that was before news broke about the thousand league beasts. What a cunning fox.

'Why didn't you tell me when I saw you before?'

'I didn't know who Cai Chong was till now,' he said innocently. 'I never read the papers.'

I had nothing to say to that. It's hard dealing with someone who lives in a cave.

—

After hanging up, I sat there blankly, still clutching my phone. I didn't dare call my professor. My eyelid was twitching so violently, I thought it might be trying to leave my face. I didn't know what he was up to, but he was capable of anything.

In my second year of university, he had an innocent young man sent to prison, then played the Good Samaritan and engineered his release, all so he could get his hands on some research materials about a species of beast. That led to my very first argument with the professor. I nearly set fire to the lab. The young man almost lost his mind in prison, and killed himself soon after his release. He left all his belongings – including the research materials, of course – to his saviour, my professor. I'd screamed that he was a terrible person, and his face sank. 'It's survival of the fittest,' he said. 'He was too weak. It's not my fault. Someone like him would have died sooner or later.'

I grabbed the folder from him and would have torn it apart, but he smacked me across the face. 'Have you lost your mind? You crazy woman. Do you know how precious this is?'

I fell to the ground. Panicking, he'd rushed over and tried to help me to my feet, but as soon as he was within range, I smacked him back. That wasn't enough. While he was still stunned, I hit him again.

He stared, then burst into laughter. He hugged me, and laughed so hard he started coughing. 'I don't know what to do with you. You were sent to test me.'

I started laughing too. We never argued again over this sort of thing.

My mother once said to me, 'You know what? Pity is useless. You might feel pity for someone if they died, but if you died, they wouldn't even look at you. Just go on living, that's the only way. Whether you're a human or a beast, just go on living.'

I didn't dare make the call.

Two hours later, the phone finally rang. It was Fei. 'The gentleman who brought the letter is back. Shall I send him up?'

I caught my breath. 'Give him the phone.'

'Hello,' said my professor. There was an anxiety in his voice I'd never heard before.

'What happened?' I laughed. 'A mountain could fall, and you wouldn't turn a hair. Is the world about to end?'

Now he laughed too. 'I want to see you,' he said.

'No.'

'Yes.' When had he become so determined?

'No.' Still laughing.

'Fine.' He hung up on me.

I blinked, and quickly called back. Busy. He hadn't put the phone down properly!

I flung on my shoes and rushed out, then darted back in for my comb. Going down in the lift, I tried to neaten my hair. Seventeen floors later, I walked out into the foyer. Fei was by the entrance, reading the paper and looking bored. 'Where's the man?' I asked.

'Just left,' said Fei, and went back to his newspaper. I fought a sudden urge to beat him to death, and rushed out into the street. The sun was so bright. Autumn was slipping away, and it was nearly winter. The street was wide and ashy white. I didn't see a single person I recognised.

This was the city I lived in: Yong'an. Its tall buildings, its magnificent streets, its prospering industries. Wanderers and exiles lived here, and no excavation would uncover anything past seven decades old. Every person here was a stranger, and the beasts were unfamiliar too. The only person I knew was so very far away. My mother had said, 'Remember the time we had together, remember that I once loved you. Then we'll part forever.'

Each day in this city, there were five hundred and thirteen traffic accidents, three hundred and twenty-eight migrant workers leaping to their deaths, seventy-eight cases of food poisoning, fifty-two rapes, and countless other suicides and attempted suicides. We never heard about the stories that didn't make it to the news – and those we did know about were never anything to do with us.

That night, I dreamed about being at university again. Like a dark joke, my professor inexplicably forced me to buy every garlic scape in the city – or he'd drop me from his classes, and I'd never graduate. Like Charlie Chaplin, I scurried around with no expression, grabbing every tin I could find. Two for the price of one, three for the price of two, no discount, marked-up, all of them went into my bag. 'Bastard,' I muttered. 'I'm spending my life savings on this. Am I going to starve or die of poverty?'

The ringing phone woke me from this nightmare. I was covered in cold sweat, but I could still laugh as I answered. It was Zhong Liang, that summer child. His voice was low, as if he'd encountered the first real difficulty in his life. 'What is it, my boy,' I crooned. 'Which little girl do you have a crush on? Or did you get kicked off a course?'

'Have you seen today's paper?' said my caveman.

'Wow.' This was new. 'Since when did you start reading the papers?'

'Go look,' he said, sounding as stern as our professor. He must have rubbed off on his young pupil. I hurried downstairs to buy a newspaper and scanned the headlines: 'Progress in Thousand League Beast Dig'; 'City Councillor Makes Speech About Spiritual Civilisation'; 'New Design for Yong'an City Coat of Arms'; 'Megastar to Hold Concert'; 'University Fees to be Devolved'…

The words blurred before my eyes. I called Zhong Liang. 'What am I looking at?'

'Page thirteen.'

'Page thirteen... "Singer Took Nude Photos Before She Was Famous..." What?'

'Rightmost column. "The News in Brief." Third line.'

It read, '... Yong'an University Zoology Professor Killed in Car Accident, Industry Insiders Say Zoology Books Suddenly in Demand Throughout Yong'an...'

'Did you see it?' Zhong Liang said. 'Did you? Hello?'

———

My editor cheerfully informed me that my book had done especially well that month, and for the first time in years, I would be on the bestseller list. 'Everyone's talking about beasts! There's so much news about them.'

'Do I get a bonus?' I asked.

'Of course, of course,' he said, falling over himself to demonstrate his benevolence. 'When will your next manuscript be ready?'

'Very soon, but I want a bigger cut of the royalties.'

'Of course,' he said hastily. 'But as for—'

I hung up on him and looked at Zhong Liang,

who was sitting across from me, dark circles under his eyes. 'Do you want to eat?' he asked.

'No.'

'I'm hungry,' he pouted.

'Then you eat,' I said tartly. 'I need to write.'

'No, you have to keep me company. You're older, you should be taking care of me.' He leaned his handsome face closer to mine.

'Fine, we'll go get some noodles.' Zhong Liang said he wanted seafood hotpot, but I said no. The noodles from the stall downstairs were famous – generously laden with meat, in a thickly fragrant sauce. I was just mixing in the sauce when I heard a loud slurping next to me. Zhong Liang had already finished his food, every scrap of it.

'Are you a hungry ghost?' I chuckled, taking a bite of my own noodles, but my stomach wasn't quite ready yet, and I spewed them out right away.

Zhong Liang jumped up with a cry of alarm. He poured me a glass of water to rinse out my mouth, then dragged me upstairs as if I were a little child. In the lift, I said, 'Zhong Liang, why are you here?'

'Where else would I be?' he said, rolling his eyes. 'One of us needs to have some sense.' What a man. I could hear the old fox in his voice.

After a while, he said, 'I still want to research

thousand league beasts.'

He looked uneasily at me, and I looked at myself in the lift doors. Silver light flickered across my reflection. My face was yellowish and devoid of expression, my eyes were dark. If my professor could have seen me like this, he'd definitely have a string of insults ready.

'Go ahead,' I said. 'Let's go and talk to Jiang Tan.'

I didn't think there was anything he could do now.

—

The trouble was, Jiang Tan was nowhere to be found. He might look innocent, but he was a slippery customer. The excavation site was completely deserted, and when I called his number, it didn't go through.

Luckily, not for nothing had Zhong Liang been our professor's pupil. He was able to dig up Jiang Tan's address.

It turned out he lived in a rubbish collection company's staff quarters to the south of the city, not far from the archaeological site. We found the place easily enough. On the seventh floor, we went past a row of doors until we found his. A middle-aged woman who looked a lot like Jiang Tan answered. 'Can I help you?'

'Is Mr Jiang in?' asked Zhong Liang.

She stared at us for a long time. 'No,' she finally said.

'When will he be back?' said Zhong Liang, unperturbed. We could wait.

'He doesn't live here.'

'Where does he live? We have urgent business to discuss with him.' Zhong Liang flashed his most charming smile, but she just glared at us, clearly unprepared to divulge any more. Finally, Zhong Liang gave up and handed her his card. 'If you hear from him, please give us a call. I'm an admirer of his, from Yong'an University.'

Nice work, I thought. *Your face didn't change at all as you were licking her boots.*

The air felt colder as we walked out. 'Let's got for a drink,' I said.

'Can I say no?' Zhong Liang said pathetically.

'No.'

—

If this were fiction, it would be far too contrived to say I saw Jiang Tan at the Dolphin Bar – but he really was there, sitting in a corner, downing glass after glass, clearly tipsy.

'How much has he had?' I murmured to the bartender, who pretended he hadn't heard.

Zhong Liang didn't care. He darted over to sit opposite Jiang Tan. 'Remember me?' he said.

'Who are you?'

'Zhong Liang.'

'Don't know you.'

'That doesn't matter.' Zhong Liang, the king of public relations, flashed a smile and poured him another drink. 'The main thing is that I know you. Have you dug up anything new?'

'We're not digging any more.'

'Why not?'

For the first time, Jiang Tan answered, like a good boy. 'Professor Cai is gone.'

'When will he be back?' I persisted.

'He's not coming back.' Jiang Tan downed his drink in one, and topped up his glass again. 'I've seen you. I remember you. But you've lost weight, haven't you?'

'My professor died,' I said.

'Mine too,' he said.

This was a shock.

'Why didn't it say so in the papers?' asked Zhong Liang suspiciously.

'It's a secret. He went after the thousand league beasts. I knew he would die. I knew it,' he muttered. 'Do you know what fate is? Fate is nine o'clock. Eight o'clock is over, and poof, it's nine o'clock. No matter what you do, or how slowly you move, you'll still get to nine.'

'You knew?' said Zhong Liang. 'Does that mean you killed him?'

'No!' Jiang Tan was agitated. 'I wanted to save him! I even killed an innocent person to save him. I thought it was a mistake, but he died. He wanted to die.'

'How could you let this happen?' To warm my icy hands, I placed them in Zhong Liang's. His eyes widened.

'I told him the person who was most precious in the world to him would die, but he couldn't tell that to the girl, we can only change our fate by hiding from it,' he babbled. Then he jumped to his feet and roared like a madman, 'I tricked him! I did! But I couldn't trick fate.'

Shaking, I tried to hold him. 'Why would he believe you? Such a clever man, why?'

Jiang Tan turned to me, his enchanting face contorted. His eyes glowed amber. Suddenly, he grinned, and lowered his mouth to my ear. 'Don't you understand?' he whispered. 'He loved her, and I'm a mongrel.' Looking into my eyes, he repeated, 'I'm a mongrel.' A tremor went through me. He let go of my hand and ran out of the bar.

I plopped down on the floor. Zhong Liang helped me up, startled by my expression. 'You're finally crying,' he said mournfully. 'I'm happy for you, but does your nose need to run too?'

I threw my arms around him and howled for our professor. This time, I would remember asking. 'I need to see him again,' I said. 'Zhong Liang, I understand why he wanted those scapes. This was all my fault!'

The year I turned eighteen, the professor had given me a watch, a limited edition with a silver face. 'You idiot,' I'd yelled at him. 'Don't you know that's bad luck? You're saying time's up.'

He looked startled, then rapped my head. 'What a lot of strange things you believe.'

I should have known. His last message to me, scrawled on the newspaper, was not A SCAPE but ESCAPE – he'd been warning me to get out.

But this had all been a trick. A lifetime of cleverness, but the one person who couldn't escape was him. Like he said, I was sent to test him.

—

Three days later, Zhong Liang came to see me. I sat at a table laden with food, waiting for him.

He sighed, 'I got the head chef of Yong'an Hotel to make this takeaway, and you're just sitting there not eating it!'

Sitting down, he cupped his chin in his hands and stared at me. 'Hey!' he said.

I jumped. 'What?'

He hesitated. 'Don't be shocked, okay? Jiang Tian's dead. He killed himself. His mum called me.'

'Should we go have a look?'

Before he could answer, I'd dragged him out the door.

—

'My son's dead,' said the woman. 'He said he was exhausted.'

We were back at the staff quarters of the rubbish collection company. The place was spotless, as if the tenement block contained no signs of life, nothing at all. She thrust a photo at us. 'Look, his father lost his mind early on. He died young, and now his son's dead too.'

Zhong Liang's eyes widened. 'Look!' He shoved it at me.

A monochrome shot from decades ago. No way to tell what colour the male beast's skin would have been, let alone his pupils, but his body was slim and upright, his hair long and black, eyes narrow, lips pale, neck long and sorrowful. There was a woman too, a beautiful one, like a female version of Jiang Tan. Jiang Tan himself sat at the couple's feet, just a child, staring coldly at the camera. His eyes were empty and melancholy, like a deceased old man.

'A thousand league beast,' said Zhong Liang hoarsely.

'I know.' I remembered, all of a sudden, the stabbing pain when his heel spur had dug into my ankle. 'He told me he was a mongrel.'

The woman took back the photo and held it to her chest. 'What did you like about my son?' she said to Zhong Liang. 'He had so many boyfriends, but it was Professor Cai he liked most. He even helped the professor find my in-laws' old house, and told him where they all went. But it turned out they're all dead. Such a shame, all dead.'

Zhong Liang smiled foolishly. 'He was beautiful, and very clever.'

'You're right,' said Jiang Tan's mother. 'He was very beautiful, and too clever. He knew everything, but he couldn't change it. What he would do today, what he would do tomorrow, every detail. Like a walking corpse, he couldn't change direction. My husband was so much luckier. He went mad, so he didn't know anything. Do you know, when my boy was at school, he got full marks in every single test...' She was no longer looking at us.

Zhong Liang couldn't stand it any longer. He gave the woman some money, grabbed my hand, and strode out. The air was still cold and dry, and still holding my hand, he abruptly let out a laugh. 'What's so funny?' I said.

'I can't blame him,' said Zhong Liang. 'Our whole lives, everything he did, all prearranged.'

I had to laugh too, when he put it like that.

'Remember the time we had together, remember that I once loved you. Then we'll part forever.' My mother's words to me.

—

Thousand league beasts see a thousand years ahead, but with all that knowledge, all they can do is walk along the path that's been laid out for them. Young beasts know everything under the sun, but cannot speak or walk. When they're grown, their memories fade and their brains weaken, until they are no different from ordinary humans. With time, their minds deteriorate further, and living becomes difficult. After ten or twenty more years, their lives end. Despite their wisdom, they come to appear foolish, and people question if they deserve such a lofty name.

Eventually, the thousand league beasts grew weary of their reputation, and spread a lie that they had gone extinct. Instead, they went underground – building houses and courtyards beneath the surface of the earth. With their amber eyes, they could see in the dark, and their swollen bellies stored air for breathing. Each time an old beast died, they moved a little further away, and now they are a thousand leagues from Yong'an.

When a human mates with one of these beasts, their child looks like the mother: a shortened body, no other markings than a sharp bone at the heel. Yet these half-beasts know the will of heaven, and will not forget with maturity. They become walking corpses, witnessing the desolation of the world, utterly alone. Eventually, they end their lives.

No one can tell from the outside if a thousand league beast has retained his wits or not.

All they can hope for is to stay alive, and to share the world with those they love, even if they are a thousand leagues away.

HEARTSICK BEASTS

The heartsick beasts are man-made creatures. More than twenty years ago, the biology department of Yong'an University announced that it had created a new beast, one with a mild temperament and an exquisite heart. Their diet consisted of steamed buns, silver fungus, and char siu pork. They made adorable pets, and would be known as heartsick beasts. This grand press conference is broadcast again every year during Yong'an's New Year concert.

Reporters from all over the world showed up in Yong'an, and their camera flashes all but blew off the roof. The young, newly appointed mayor and the even younger inventor unveiled a video of the beast: a young one, its face still not fully formed, smooth as an eggshell, with slits where the eyes and nose would be. It was just learning to speak. It had powdery-white skin and inky-black hair. A female beast. Everyone loved her. The attendants fed her char siu, mashed potato, and orange juice. She devoured it all, like the wind scooping up ragged clouds. Another video showed her fully grown two months later, her eyes large and dark, her nose straight, exactly like a human child. Astonishment swept through the audience.

The young academic shot to fame, and was put in charge of the zoology department at Yong'an University.

He was my professor.

—

But all of that happened a long while back, more than twenty years ago, and much has changed since. These days, you can buy a heartsick beast on the seventh floor of Yong'an's largest shopping centre, Heavenly Beauty Mall. They cost 88,800 yuan each, and don't bother asking for a discount. Ordinary people wouldn't dare dream of acquiring one, but there's no shortage of rich folk heartsick enough to open their wallets. The young beasts float in tanks of formaldehyde, their bodies perfectly smooth and flawless, male and female for the choosing, a blank where their face should be.

The shop attendants create a meticulous menu based on what appearance the customer requests. Day one: three grams of sardine for a straight nose, thirty grams of stewed tofu for cuteness, char siu for beautiful eyes, and a char siu bun for single eyelids. Then different quantities of different foods on day two, and again for every day after that, schematic as a computer programme. After three months, the beast will have grown to the size of a five-year-old human, its vocabulary and intelligence similarly accelerated to keep pace with your child and stave off loneliness. Heartsick beasts have an outsize ability to foster morality and develop intellect, and any child growing up in the company of one is sure to become a pillar of society. After five years of use, the company recycles the beasts, so they don't become a burden on your family. During your time with the beast, the company sends you an annual present: four sets of all-weather outfits, and a three-month supply of tinned beast food. After recycling, you get another small gift: a hamper of health food, a family studio portrait, and a set of CD-ROMs – great value. More treats at Christmas: a full set of Good Baby bath supplies, and a chance to win a South East Asia trip for your entire family.

During our phone call, my cousin recited the advertisement copy to me as if she'd had a stroke, battering my eardrums with her noble mother-love. 'Are you going to get one?' I asked. 'They're not cheap.'

'Lucia's about to start primary school,' said my cousin. 'This is a bit of an investment, but it's totally worth it. These five years are crucial for her development!'

So she'd already been completely brainwashed. Feeling helpless, all I could do was ask, 'Do you really believe everything they say in that ad?'

'I don't just follow people blindly,' said my cousin defensively. 'Their statistics are ironclad. Heartsick beasts are nothing but beneficial for children.'

I had nothing to say to that. She wasn't telling me anything new – the most important officials, big-shot business leaders and famous artists of Yong'an City, had indeed had heartsick beasts as children. Also 85.7% of high-ranking executives, at the very least.

'What about the other 14.3%?' I persisted.

A roar came down the line. 'Do you really think my daughter could be that useless?'

'You're right, you're right.' Having trodden on a tiger mum's tail, I had no choice but to beat a frantic retreat. 'I was just worried about your husband's hard-earned money. Why are you asking me, anyway, if you've already made up your mind?'

'I want you to take Lucia to pick one out this Sunday, of course. Luckily you studied zoology for a couple of years. And didn't the person who invented them teach in your department? Do you know him?'

'Yes, I knew him.'

'Are you close?' she asked, then let out an anguished yelp. 'Oh right, he died recently. Shame, otherwise I'd have got you to ask him for a discount...'

'It wouldn't have had anything to do with him – the government procured the rights long ago,' I calmly informed her.

My cousin finished with a stream of meaningless small talk that concluded with, 'All right then, we'll see you at Heavenly Beauty Mall this Sunday. Front entrance, half-past nine.'

—

The sun was bright that Sunday, and Lucia's smile even more radiant, which swiftly smoothed over the psychological assault of my cousin's magenta jacket embroidered with gold thread. The girl lunged over to hug me. 'Auntie!' she cried.

No wonder people have kittens or puppies or little children. This felt nice.

My bones softened and I scooped her up to plant a vigorous kiss on her cheek. Lucia made a sudden grab for my face and turned it this way and that. 'Why are you so skinny, Auntie? You look like you haven't been eating.'

It was enough to bring me close to tears. I would have done anything for her.

We went to the seventh floor, which had been done up to look like a mad scientist's lab. If these commerce-minded parasites could have actually seen my professor's lab, the one I'd repeatedly vandalised, they'd surely have vomited blood. We chose a female beast for Lucia, though there wasn't actually much choice: the entire row of beasts looked exactly the same, the faces smooth as eggs, with dots to mark where their eyes and nose would be, and a line for the mouth. They floated in individual jars, like some sort of pickles.

My cousin gritted her teeth and handed over her credit card; her hand shook as she signed the receipt. All the humanity had drained from her face, but at least she got a jar out of it. Lucia seemed alarmed by the tiny beast. 'Is she really alive, Auntie?' she asked.

'Not yet,' I said. 'In a moment they'll take her out and give her an injection to wake her up.'

'Oh...' Lucia leaned closer, pupils narrowing as she stared, rapt. The jar seemed like something from a perfectly still universe where nothing had happened yet. Terra nullius.

The attendant brought over a folder of documents for my cousin to fill in, then turned to Lucia with a smile like a gardenful of flowers. 'What would you like her to look like, my little friend?'

Lucia finally looked away from the jar, and up at the three adults. 'Like Auntie,' she said. My cousin's face darkened. She would happily have murdered me a thousand times over.

Traitor that I was, I pulled back like a tortoise retreating into its shell, and muttered, 'Wouldn't you rather she looked like your mummy?'

'No.' The girl was adamant. 'Like Auntie.'

'Lucia…'

My cousin pinched me hard, smiling. 'All right, we'll have her look like your aunt.'

The attendant led me into a photo booth where a blinding flash went off, *kchaa kchaa kchaa* – front, side, and back – as if I were a convict.

These photos were fed into a computer that spat out a sheaf of recipes moments later. The attendant nimbly bound these into a little booklet, and handed them to my cousin. 'Feed your beast according to these instructions. If any issues come up, just bring her back to be fixed.' Then another attendant came over holding the beast, who'd now had her injection, and was dressed in the clothes of a human infant. Swaddled as she was, her chest was clearly rising and falling as she breathed through the nostril holes on her face. Lucia snatched her tight and said, 'Look, my baby.'

At the sight of her daughter's delight, my cousin finally relaxed and stopped glaring at me.

We said goodbye in the foyer. Somewhere on the way down, the beast had been named Lulu. Lucia hugged her tight and said, 'Auntie, come visit me and Lulu next week!'

I hadn't helped at all, and now my cousin was cross with me. I kept my mouth shut out of fear, looking sidelong at her until she relented. 'Fine, yes, come round.'

All but falling to my knees, I answered, 'At your service!' And then we parted.

—

Christmas was almost upon us. The streets were brightly decorated, and the lonely grew lonelier. I'd planned to go home, but changed my mind halfway there and went to the Dolphin Bar instead. Zhong Liang was hunched over like a caveman, guzzling beer. When he saw me, he launched himself at me like Lucia, and yelled, 'I'm in love!'

I steadied him and sat down, trying not to laugh. Despite everything that was going on, I managed to order myself a pint before asking him, 'Who is she?'

'The woman of my dreams!' An unexpectedly florid answer.

I almost throttled him.

Everyone there, including the bartender, was looking at me with pity, and from their twitching faces I could tell I wasn't the first victim that evening. Zhong Liang swung towards me like a sumo wrestler, ready to regale me with his account of falling into the river of love.

'... I've been dreaming about her every night... I wake up feeling so happy... Hey! Don't look at me like that, I've seen her in real life, I swear, I've definitely met her before... But for some reason, I can't remember where... She must be somewhere, maybe even here in Yong'an...'

I cursed myself for walking into this hell instead of going home when I had the chance. Now I was forced to soothe him as if he were a little dog. 'Maybe she's a distant relative?'

'I described her to my mum and dad, and they said we aren't related to anyone like that,' he said in despair.

'What are you going to do, then?'

'I have to find her!' He vowed, taking my hand as if I were the unfortunate woman swimming alongside him in the river of love. 'I have an intuition that she must still be in Yong'an. I won't rest until I find her!'

'Okay, so go find her.' I retrieved my hand and

took a sip of beer.

'So you'll come with me?' He almost flung himself at me. 'Thank you!'

'What?' I turned to see the entire bar was staring at me, the same three words flashing from their collective eyes: *serves you right*.

———

I'd hoped Zhong Liang would somehow forget the whole thing overnight, but of course that was wishful thinking – he was far too full of energy. According to him, he'd dreamt of her again. 'We were having a meal together. It was such bliss. She put a piece of carrot on my plate, and said carrots make your eyes shine. She's so sweet...' Countless tiny stars appeared in his eyes.

I couldn't bear to look, so I pulled the covers over my head, but he bounded over and ripped them off. 'Get up! We have to go find her!'

I yelped piteously, cursing my professor: *so you're dead, couldn't you rest in peace instead of lumbering me with your deranged protégé?* I accepted my fate and got out of bed. As soon as I'd washed and dressed, Zhong Liang dragged me through the door, in search of his dream maiden.

It being Monday, the streets were a little desolate.

Zhong Liang set a frenetic pace, and I had to ask, 'Where are we going?'

'Police station.'

'What, are you planning to go through all their files?'

'If you have money, you can make the devil himself do your bidding.' Being born with a silver spoon in his mouth, Zhong Liang naturally saw the world differently from me. And indeed, the deputy chief of police was waiting to greet us at the front entrance. He ushered us in, served us tea, and kept asking, 'Are you doing well, sir?' The effect was hypnotic. The small talk took quite a while, then we finally got down to business.

I waited for Zhong Liang in the corridor, like a hooker who'd been swept up in a vice raid. Even with my thick woollen hat on, it was cold in there, so I lit up a cigarette to keep warm. My lighter began to run out of fuel, and I had to click it quite a few times to coax out a flame. Even then, my hands trembled. I'd dropped five cigarettes before Zhong Liang finally appeared, handing over the photofit he'd assembled as if it was some sort of treasure. 'This is her,' he said, trying to sound mysterious but unable to hide his excitement.

I looked at the photo. Even as a mechanical

reproduction, this woman was supernaturally beautiful. She would stand out in any crowd. Her liquid eyes were bewitching.

I stared for a moment, then burst out laughing. 'I know her,' I said.

'You do?' His face changed. He looked like he might have taken a bite out of me. 'Who is she?'

I pulled him closer, and whispered into his ear. 'I've got a picture of her at home. Come back with me and I'll show you.'

He looked at me and, as if he'd been spellbound. 'All right.'

We said goodbye to the overly friendly deputy, and headed to my flat. Zhong Liang didn't say a word the whole way, just clutched the composite picture tight, his head lowered. I noticed sweat beading across his brows.

This was difficult to bear, but I didn't say anything. I let him in, told him to take a seat, made him a cup of tea, then slowly went to the study to get a book. His eyes followed me, full of hope and despair.

I set the book before him and he eagerly opened it. A ripped-out bit of old newspaper that had been sandwiched between the pages fell out, most of it taken up by an enormous headline: 'Film Star Lin Bao Kills Self!!!' Three exclamation marks. Below that was a photo; the woman in it was a little older, but otherwise it was the exact image of the woman of his dreams.

He stared at her, mouth gaping. I couldn't help laughing. 'You must have been an early bloomer, Zhong Liang. Lin Bao died when you were, what, eleven or twelve? I don't know how you saw her picture, but to think you're still dreaming of her after so many years. Adorable.' I chuckled away, but he didn't move, just stared at the scrap of paper, brows still furrowed. I went over and tapped him on the shoulder. 'Hey, don't worry, I'm not going to tell anyone. I just think it's cute.'

'No!' He snapped back to himself. 'That's not right. The girl in my dreams is young, seven or eight. The photofit is what I thought she'd look like when she'd grow up. It couldn't be this woman. If she was already this age when I was a boy, wouldn't she be an old hag by now?'

After his rant, he had the nerve to roll his eyes at me.

How dare he.

'Paedo!' I spat at him.

'The girl would be about my age by now,' he retorted. 'How does that make me a paedo?'

I stared at him for a good long while, until my

196 Strange Beasts of China

anger turned back to laughter. 'Okay, okay,' I said, hauling him to his feet. 'Go look for her yourself, then!' I shoved him out the door. Finally, peace for my ears.

What a lunatic. Pig-headed, just like our professor.

Now he was gone, I sat down with a cup of coffee and had a look at the old newspaper. In the column to the left of the picture was a short news item: **After a fire broke out in the Temple of the Antiquities yesterday, fire services report that the blaze was quickly and efficiently brought under control. Officials note that a woman's body was found afterwards; however, the cause of death was determined to be an existing illness. Thanks to the quick intervention of the fire brigade, the temple suffered no other damage, and was just as full of worshippers today.**

A laugh escaped me as I put down the paper. All my life, whenever I lost someone dear to me, the news would be covered like this: a few blocks of tofu on the page. Contrast that with Lin Bao, who'd lived so splendidly. She smiled up at me, her dimples like blossoms now long withered away.

My mother had said, 'You're only alive for a while, but dead forever. How you live, how you die, that's your own business.'

I didn't know how she died. 'None of your

business,' she would have said.

I shut my eyes. It was so cold. I gulped down my coffee, but it didn't help. Sleep swept over me. I glimpsed my professor through bleary eyes. He patted my head and said, 'You're adorable. It makes me happy to look at you.'

I wanted to smile. When had he ever treated me so kindly? But I couldn't smile. Finally, I slept.

—

Before we got to Sunday, my cousin phoned, her voice shaking from excitement. 'I won!'

'Won what?' I was confused.

'A prize!' What little patience my cousin had, I'd taught her. 'A family holiday – four days in South East Asia!'

'Oh!' I'd forgotten about the heartsick beast raffle. 'Are you sure?'

'Of course! You think I didn't double-check the numbers? We leave tomorrow – you'll have to take care of Lulu. Come round tonight. But I warn you, she's become the darling of our family. Feed her exactly according to the manual. If you get it wrong, I'll hack you to pieces.'

This was such a bombardment of information, it took me a moment to grasp the main point. 'Wait!' I wailed. 'Isn't there anyone else you could ask?'

'Aren't you a zoologist?'

There wasn't much I could say to that. 'Our syllabus didn't cover feeding pets,' I tried feebly, but her highness had already hung up.

—

I picked up the little beast that evening. After just a week, she had grown eyebrows, her eyes half-open. There was a little bump where her nose would be, and her ears were protruding a little, like white fungus. Still in her swaddling, she had matured quite a bit. I carefully took her in my arms, like a precious object. Lucia tugged at my hand, tears in her eyes. 'Take good care of Lulu, Auntie.'

'I will,' I said. 'Four days isn't long.' Even so, I thought my head would fall off from all the instructions they lobbed in my direction before finally releasing me.

I didn't dare walk with Lulu. In the taxi home, I studied the little beast with a tickle in my heart. Would she really grow up to look like me? I touched her index finger, long and soft, and she smiled at me. Just like a human baby.

I had a sudden thought, and phoned Zhong Liang. 'Where are you? I know who your dream woman is.'

'As if I'd believe you,' he sneered.

'Really!' I blurted out. 'She's not human.'

He swore and was about to hang up, so I quickly said, 'No, listen! She's a heartsick beast.'

'A beast?' At least he was still on the line.

'Yes,' I said, 'You know the ones I'm talking about. You must have had one of those, when you were a child.'

He was silent for a while. Just as I started to wonder if he'd died from shock, he said, 'Where are you now? I'll come to you.'

———

Back at my flat, Zhong Liang stared at the little beast as if she were a panda, and reached out tentatively to touch her face. 'Oh please!' I said. 'You studied in the same lab as me, don't act like you're some kind of alien. It's embarrassing.'

'We never researched heartsick beasts,' he said. 'The professor wouldn't let us.'

I felt the generation gap yawning between us. 'How much do you know about them?'

'About as much as anyone else,' he said innocently.

That was too humble; the correct answer was that he knew nothing at all. Time for some labour. I painstakingly explained these beasts to him, and he said, looking thunderstruck, 'You mean they can look like anyone at all?'

'Yes,' I said, feeling all my strength draining away. 'Have you never seen that film they screen every New Year?'

'My family always goes abroad at New Year.'

I took a deep breath, and cut to the conclusion. 'I believe the woman of your dreams is a heartsick beast you had as a child. Probably she watched too much TV, and grew up to look like Lin Bao.'

'That's impossible! My parents would have known about that. This must be a pretty girl I saw when I was a child. A human girl. And she's waiting for me somewhere.'

I couldn't be bothered with any more of his nonsense, so once again, I just shoved him out of my flat. 'Talk to your parents,' I said.

Once he was gone, I followed the feeding instructions and gave the little beast twenty grams of milk, five grams of shrimp, ten grams of mango – carefully measuring each portion out using industrial scales, just like a scientist. The beast played in my arms for a while, then dozed off. I put her to bed, and went back to the living room to read the papers.

This was a habit I'd formed after my professor died. Each day, I'd buy every newspaper this city had to offer, big ones and small ones. No news item was too insignificant. I even read the matrimonial ads. Finally, I felt myself grow as wise as Zhuge Liang, who knew everything there was to know without leaving his thatched hut.

The papers that day mostly led with an outbreak of unrest in a tropical region of South East Asia, the result of excessively hot weather. People had taken to the streets, eyes red with anger, getting into brawls and looting shops. A well-known commentator wrote a column on the topic 'The Rebirth of Bestial Nature', bestowing his opinion for the enlightenment of all and sundry, touching on philosophy, sociology and anthropology, writing with great flair, more quotes than text. I sighed. I knew that's how it would be – the things I read in the papers never had anything to do with me.

Every story is someone else's myth. Life holds no pleasant surprises for us, only nasty shocks.

When my mother died, Third Aunt saw the news in the paper and came looking for me at the Temple of the Antiquities, exclaiming, 'You're getting to look more and more like your mother! Really, just like her!' She took me home, and I wept all the way. At her house, I met my cousin for the first time. She was a year older than me, in sixth form. Her hair was in two little pigtails, and she wore a red dress. She was playing a video game rather than doing her homework. Third Aunt said, 'Come quick, this is your little cousin.' She glanced at me and said, 'Huh, she looks more like my big cousin.'

I had to laugh. That's how she'd always been, direct and tactless. Third Aunt wrapped her arms around me and sobbed, 'Lucky I read the newspaper, otherwise I wouldn't have known your mum was gone. I saw her at the temple just the year before – wasn't she perfectly fine then? I know she was adopted, but we always got on so well, from when we were little children...'

My cousin pulled me aside and snapped at her mother, 'Stop talking, can't you see she's tired? You should be letting her rest, not going on about this old nonsense.'

Instead of getting angry, Third Aunt agreed abjectly. I was surprised. After all, I was still young, and envied my cousin having a family like this.

My cousin was too coarse to understand the tender feelings swirling around inside me, and dragged me off to play with her. 'What video games do you like?' she asked.

We studied together. Grinning, she ordered me to do her homework. 'You're such a genius, sis, you're already in secondary school. Help me write this essay.'

I clutched the newspaper now, my mind travelling thousands of miles. This was all in the past, heretical teachings.

Third Aunt died the year I got into university. Before she passed away, she clutched my arm and said, 'At least I can face your mother now!' And then she departed.

It was an unquiet night in Yong'an. Someone was setting off fireworks – it was almost Christmas, after all.

This city is permanently cold. Those who leave go in search of some place warmer.

—

Another day passed. Zhong Liang turned up at my door before dawn, and presented me with a basket of apples. 'Happy Christmas,' he said.

I stared at him suspiciously, completely dishevelled and still half asleep. 'I don't believe you've come here first thing in the morning just to wish me a happy Christmas,' I said.

Zhong Liang laughed foolishly. 'Nothing gets past you, I see.' Even as he flattered me, he was stepping into my flat, not bothering to take off his shoes, and plopping down directly in a chair. 'Let's go to the heartsick beast factory.'

'What? So you believe me now?' I smiled frostily.

'I went back home and asked my mum and dad yesterday...'

'And they remembered?'

'No, they still won't admit it, but they were behaving strangely. I think they must be hiding something from me, so I'd like to go have a look at the factory.'

'So?' I slouched on the sofa, ready to doze off.

'I want you to come with me!' He dragged me roughly to my feet. This was no way to treat a lady, this boy showed no respect for his elders.

Christmas gave the illusion that the whole city was full of joy. Zhong Liang drove us there. The news blared on the car radio: the strange outbursts of rage were getting harder and harder to control. Since the initial explosion in the tropical region, the violence had been spreading steadily. Locally, thirteen city administrations had been occupied by rioters, who now sat sobbing hysterically in the council chambers. Experts carried out research and concluded that eating raw garlic could dampen this anger.

Zhong Liang let out a bitter laugh. Anything that took place in a lush tropical jungle felt like a happy adventure story, without any overtones of tragedy. He turned to me. 'Have you tried eating raw garlic?'

Instead of rising to the bait, I asked, 'My cousin and her family are in South East Asia. Do you think they'll be all right?'

'No,' he said, nonchalantly. 'It's chaos over there. They should come back as soon as they can. Or if they can't, they should take shelter at our embassy.'

I stared out the window, my heart starting and stopping. Zhong Liang said, 'Don't tell me you already had some raw garlic this morning?' I smacked his arm, which seemed to satisfy him, and he stopped needling me.

Half an hour later, we were past the third ring road, and then at the heartsick beast factory. Zhong Liang made a call, and used his father's name to get us seen right away by the customer service manager, who turned out to be a bad-tempered man with terrible garlicky breath (implying that he was keeping up with current events). We frowned and pulled away from him. Safely at the far side of the manager's desk, Zhong Liang asked, 'Could you look in your files and tell me if you ever had a client named Zhong Kui?'

That name was a thunderbolt. Mr Zhong Kui, Zhong Liang's father, was a big deal in this city. His business empire spanned construction, communications, exports, manufacturing, and pharmaceuticals, and he'd appeared on the *Forbes* list. One of his ancestors was a famous general from the early days of Yong'an, and his family tree was studded with an astonishing list of accomplishments on both sides of the law.

The little manager leaned towards us, almost pressing his face to Zhong Liang's, and nodding. 'Of course, of course, that's no problem at all.' A quick search produced the information that Zhong Liang's father had – unsurprisingly – bought a heartsick beast, ten years ago. Zhong Liang would have been in secondary school then. His grades were poor, and he'd fallen into bad company. His father had purchased one of the more intelligent female beasts in the hopes that she would nurture a loving heart, and urge young Zhong Liang to be a better student.

Zhong Liang's eyes shone. 'Where is she now?' he asked the manager.

'I don't know.'

'What?' roared Zhong Liang.

'I don't know,' the manager stubbornly repeated, beginning to sweat.

'I want to speak to your boss.' Flames were practically shooting from Zhong Liang's ears.

'The boss won't know either, Mr Zhong. This comes under government jurisdiction.'

I tugged at Zhong Liang's hand. 'Let's go.'

He stared at me for a few seconds, and understood that this conversation would go nowhere. 'Fine, let's go.'

As we walked out, I shot the little manager a look, calculated to give him recurrent bouts of anxiety for at least three months.

—

Zhong Liang was in an even greater state of terror than the manager. Our local media was reporting the ongoing violence in the tropical state with all the gusto of a crowd watching a house burn down while safely on the other side of a wall. 'They even had suicide bombers!', the media relayed, while reminding listeners that chewing on raw garlic could help them keep their emotions under control. Now there were more and more people walking around with bad breath, and the whole thing seemed like a bit of a ruse.

'This is ridiculous,' said Zhong Liang. 'Even if you're in a bad mood, you can't just start eating raw garlic. What is everyone thinking? Has the whole world gone mad?'

Yong'an's local government probably benefited most from the media's mass assault, particularly after the *Yong'an Daily* ran a front-page piece urging a citywide public morality campaign. The first item on their agenda implored citizens to consume raw garlic at least twice a day.

Zhong Liang and I ran for our lives, staying far away from everyone else. 'We might as well be in a madhouse,' he fumed.

We were walking down a narrow street when he suddenly grinned.

'What are you smiling about?' I asked. The two of us were ambling alone on this long road, and although an onlooker might have assumed we were on a date, there was no reason to be this happy.

'I wonder what she's doing,' he said, his face full of tenderness, a picture of true love.

I knew he was talking about the heartsick beast, that childhood playmate of his who'd become the woman of his dreams. 'How could I forget,' he said, 'When Dad brought her home, she looked like a five-year-old, a pretty little girl. She walked over and called me "brother". Dad said, "This is your little sister. Make sure you treat her nicely."

'She was like a little porcelain doll. Right away, I was fond of her. She didn't like to go out, so I stayed home too. She enjoyed reading, and I kept her company. Even at that juvenile age, she was very clever and well-spoken. She'd always beat me at chess.

'Then she suddenly vanished. I forgot her. What's she doing now? Where is she?'

In this desolate city, he was missing his heartsick beast: a man-made creation, sold at a high price, the best companion for any child. None of these facts mattered to him. He walked by my side, eyes shaded, full of anxiety. Still so handsome. 'Where has she gone?' he said.

'Do you think she's all right?'

I sighed and took his hand. 'Stop worrying,' I said.

'I miss her, but I'm not worried. Maybe it's better if she's dead. She'll never get hurt again, not even if there's violence or war or widespread halitosis. None of those things can hurt her. I just miss her.'

—

I went back home and fed Lucia's heartsick beast: three grams of carrot, ten grams of water, ten grams of Coca-Cola. She didn't seem hungry, and threw up halfway through the meal. 'Are you worried too?' I tweaked her little newly sprouted nose. Tiny as it was, you could already tell it was going to look just like mine.

I went to bed, and was startled awake in the middle of the night by the phone ringing.

It was Lucia. 'Auntie...' was all she managed to say,

before my cousin snatched the receiver.

'We're stuck at the airport,' she said.

'Hmm?' I said sleepily. 'How's that?'

'We're stuck at the airport! Things are such a mess, we had to leave before we had the chance to really enjoy ourselves. Now we're at Yong'an Airport, but they're holding us here. We're not allowed to enter the city.' My cousin sounded frantic – there was a catch in her voice.

Now her husband took the phone and said, 'Don't worry, we'll be fine. It's probably just a preventive measure. After all, it was really chaotic over there. Only thing is, Lucia's overtired and won't settle. Can you calm her down?'

Then the phone went back to Lucia. A little dazed by this round of pass-the-telephone, I heard her say, 'Auntie, is Lulu all right?'

'Yes, she's doing great!' I said. 'Lucia, you'll need to be a brave little girl. Don't be scared. You can come home tomorrow. I'll make you braised pork.'

'No! I want chicken wings in Coca-Cola.' Lucia was a picky eater.

'Sure, all right.'

'I miss you, Auntie.' Now she'd got what she wanted, she was prepared to dispense some affection.

'I miss you too,' I said.

We chatted for another five or six minutes, then Lucia hung up.

The heartsick beast was in bed, uttering muffled sounds, brows knitted. She clutched at my fingers. 'Are you worried about Lucia?' I asked.

She mumbled something. I thought I saw tears in her eyes.

I hugged her. She was soft and warm. 'It's all right, you silly thing,' I said. 'Don't worry, they'll be back.'

—

When it got to the next day, thought, they still weren't back.

'Returning Tourists Euthanised at Airport?' screamed the newspaper headlines. Everyone was scared of unrest erupting, spreading like a contagion, and it was said that the government had decided to sacrifice a small number of people for the greater good. In order to keep Yong'an safe from the taint of violence, and to preserve our ranking in the Ten Most Civilised Cities, everyone returning from the riot zone would be put to sleep.

I phoned Zhong Liang. 'Have they brought April Fool's forward to December?'

'This is no joke,' he said sombrely.

There was a huge protest in Yong'an. A crowd

marched boldly on City Hall, humans and beasts inter-mingled, office workers, businessmen and women, and civil servants. A sea of bodies – adults, youths, and even children – resplendent in their brightly coloured clothes, all of them waving banners and chanting, 'Good behaviour in Yong'an! Politeness, not violence! Make them disappear!' Images of one disaster after another in the tropical country flashed onto a giant screen: slaughter in the streets, robbery at gunpoint, enraged rioters storming parliament and snatching the wigs off ministers' heads, each wave adding momentum to the next, until it seemed the entire world was in chaos.

There was a small counter-protest, a few hardy souls holding up placards: 'Don't kill the innocent!' The crowd engulfed them, and in an instant, they were gone.

Looking down from my flat, I thought this city had never seemed so orderly. Every single person was shouting the same slogans in unison, feeling the same fears, breathing the same destiny. Their faces were green from fear, their hands trembling. This was a place of madness. The best and brightest of Yong'an, its most essential workers, were the force behind this movement. As for the rest of us – vagrants and fugitives, peasants and artists – we looked on from a distance. Soon we, too, would be swallowed whole.

I phoned my cousin but couldn't get through. Over and over, the recorded voice told me: *The number you have called does not exist.*

Does not exist.

Our city was undergoing some kind of collective meltdown. As with any other outbreak of violence, large numbers gave the crowd a sort of magnificence, while the few voices of doubt or confusion were quickly stamped out. Clearly, the protestors weren't actually mad, and lunatics don't automatically start rioting. Rather, an unknown power was whispering: *Go ahead, be crazy. Everyone's crazy.*

The same voice said: *Make them disappear.* And they disappeared.

They would die – I knew this with utter clarity. This was no joke, the city was in the grip of madness. Now what? Now what? My cousin, her husband and little Lucia were all trapped at the airport, waiting to be euthanised.

I paced back and forth in my flat, wishing I could just put my head through a window. The leaders of this movement were unassailably high up, practically deities. Anyone who they said should die, would die. And they had the voices of countless lunatics from all across Yong'an backing them up.

I instinctively picked up my phone. Being all-powerful, my professor could surely help me out with a single call. As long as those three could be spared, I didn't care about anyone else.

Just before I dialled, I remembered he was dead, and burst into loud sobs.

My professor was dead, and all he'd left me was that annoying boy Zhong Liang... oh!

Of course, I knew more than one all-powerful person. I quickly called Zhong Liang and blurted out, 'I need your help. My cousin and her family are being held at the airport. Ask your father to get them released!'

He seemed startled. 'My dad was just cursing those people – he thinks they've all gone mad. Don't cry, please don't cry. I'll have a word with him, it'll be fine. Where are you now? Come over to mine, don't sit there brooding on your own.'

His voice was stern, just like my professor's when he called me an idiot, the same rhythms.

I didn't hesitate. 'Yes, all right,' I said, over and over.

'Bring the heartsick beast!' he ordered.

'Yes.' I darted into the bedroom, where I'd left Lulu. Lucia's little beast, the one who was supposed to look just like me.

I froze.

'Hello?' Zhong Liang sounded agitated. 'What's wrong? What's happened? Hello?'

The beast was in bed, but her chest was still. Her clothes were smeared with vomit, a mishmash of colours, impossible to tell from what food. The pale skin of her face had been ripped to shreds by her own claws. She was unrecognisable.

'A little beast like my little aunt,' Lucia had said. 'My Lulu!'

Everything went black.

In the darkness, I saw my professor. His temper was much improved, now that he'd died. He patted my shoulder and said, 'Don't be scared, this will all be over soon. You'll be absolutely fine, my precious darling.'

To think such tawdry words could ever come from his mouth.

—

I woke up in bed. I whipped my head around, but there was nothing beside me, and the covers were clean. Zhong Liang sat across from me. He let out a sigh of relief and said, 'You're awake.'

'The heartsick beast?' I asked.

'Dead.' He was preternaturally calm.

'88,800 yuan! My cousin's going to strangle me. My cousin... Zhong Liang!' I exclaimed. 'What happened to my cousin?'

'The council just held an emergency vote about the euthanasia. It passed almost unanimously. Only one vote against...'

'They're insane!' I didn't know if I should cry or start swearing. 'Who voted against it?'

'My dad,' he said proudly.

I smiled grimly.

I turned on the TV. The finance channel, the movie channel, the news channel, all playing as usual, nothing out of order. But I knew the city was transfixed by insanity. Our mayor wept as he said, 'Our only choice is to kill them. They will be the tragic heroes of Yong'an! We must smother this outbreak of violence in the cradle, to preserve our zero crime rate.'

Deafening applause, as if the entire audience was hypnotised.

Zhong Liang saw me turn pale. 'Don't worry,' he said. 'I've spoken to my dad. He'll find a way to get them out. I phoned earlier, and he said it was all going well. Let's go back to my place and wait.'

I was at his mercy.

'Let's go,' I said, but when I tried to stand up, my

head spun, and he had to reach out to steady me. 'What the hell?' he said, frowning. 'Your body's falling apart.'

'Look who's talking,' I said.

—

Zhong Liang lived in the poshest district of Yong'an, a terrifying place covered in fascist slogans: *Build a Civilised Society! Have Better People as your Neighbours!* It was all so nonsensical, I wondered if I was still dreaming.

At least Zhong Liang's house was free of this rubbish. Mr Zhong Kui came out to greet us. You could tell right away he was a great man – from his height and sleek figure, his distinctive bearing, and his unconventional manner. Such a shame about his lofty name, I thought to myself.

Mrs Zhong was quite an oil painting herself. She smiled elegantly as she waved me to a seat and poured tea. 'Your cousin and her family will be with you in no time at all.' She said this casually – clearly nothing ever ruffled her.

Mr Zhong Kui began with some small talk. 'I've read your novels...' he said.

An alarming opening. My scalp seized up, and I said, flustered, 'I'll be sure to send you my next one.'

He laughed heartily. 'That won't do – you can hardly go around giving everyone a copy. I'll buy it for myself.'

We chatted for a while, then the conversation turned to the protest in support of a more civilised society. Mr Zhong Kui sighed, 'After those governments were overthrown in South East Asia, things got a bit sensitive over here. People are holding on to personal grudges… And to think the message resonated with so many people. Unbelievable!' He had to laugh at his own words. 'It's hard to blame them, though. Yong'an is famous for getting all its motions passed unanimously. Normally that's fine, but to play around at a time like this – it really is deranged.'

I stared at him, and involuntarily shuddered. 'Yes, someone's definitely crazy. The question is, is it them or us?'

'Who knows? What human or beast could answer that?'

'There was a change in the air overnight,' I said. 'Even my niece's heartsick beast died just yesterday.'

At the words 'heartsick beast', Zhong Liang let out a vigorous cough, and Mrs Zhong flinched, but no one said anything.

We sat awkwardly for a while, until we heard the patter of footsteps, and Lucia's voice calling, 'Auntie,

Auntie!'

Then my cousin and her husband came in, and we held hands, saying nothing. The silence spoke louder than any words could.

I was nearly blinded by tears, but my cousin's glares jolted me back to reality. After we had thanked the Zhongs fulsomely, Zhong Liang announced that he would give us a lift home.

Our first stop was my cousin's flat. She asked if I wanted to come up, but I said no, I was too tired. I still hadn't found a way to tell them about the heart-sick beast. They were exhausted too. We would deal with it the next day.

We said goodbye, and Zhong Liang and I drove off. After a long silence, Zhong Liang said, 'Please don't mention the heartsick beasts again.'

'Why not?'

'I asked my parents about it, and they had a godawful argument. Turns out my dad bought the beast and asked for it to look like Lin Bao. He pretended it was for me, but after a year or so, my mum found out that he and Lin Bao used to be lovers, and she forced him to send it back. They fought hard about it, and now my mum loathes heartsick beasts. The firm sent all sorts of gifts afterwards, sofas and tinned food and whatnot, and she threw them all away without a second glance.'

I looked at him carefully, but his attention was on the road. I had to laugh. So that was the story of the rich man and the film star who'd killed herself.

'That said,' Zhong Liang went on, 'I don't know where that particular heartsick beast ended up. Maybe no one wanted her after she was sent back, so they killed her off.'

There was no expression on his face, but his knuckles were white as he gripped the steering wheel.

'They wouldn't do that,' I consoled him. 'So many people buy heartsick beasts – I'm sure every child in your neighbourhood had one. They couldn't kill them all. What would they do with the bodies? Eat th—?'

I bit off the last word, and Zhong Liang hit the brakes. He turned to me, face chalk-white. 'You mean...'

'It was him!' Just like that, I understood everything. There was nothing he wasn't capable of.

My professor had got what he wanted by unfair means. But why? What did he want? Why turn Yong'an into a city of madness?

Heartsick beasts. Why call them that? Now I knew. Heartsick. Sick at heart.

We stopped by the side of the road for a very

long time. I grew cold all over. Finally, Zhong Liang started the car again. We drove over a bridge, and as we rounded the highest point, the lights of the city spread out below us. My cousin and her family had returned, but many more people would be executed.

Their faces would be bland as they greeted you politely with a smile. Walking corpses. In the faraway south, that scorching place, governments were being overthrown and citizens slaughtered. None of that had anything to do with us. Anyone involved was long gone. And I knew that after this was all over, all these reports would vanish into thin air like ghosts. The halitotic crowds would vanish too, and grudges would be worked out to nothing. There'd be nothing left at all.

We'd forget this ever happened, all of us. If anyone happened to remember, the memories would slowly fade.

Lunatics, every single one.

—

I couldn't sleep that night. I sat staring at the newspaper I'd kept, a little square announcing his death. The hand of god tucked in a corner, a lonely child behind him. Who could have known that in death, he'd change everyone?

It's a good thing he's dead. The thought flashed through my head.

Once again, I cried.

Christmas was over, and the sky above the city was pitch-dark. Everyone I knew was asleep, but some strangers were dead.

—

The next day, I confessed to my cousin. 'I've let you down,' I said. 'I'll work hard till I've saved up the money to pay you back. Lulu's dead.'

My cousin received the news with equanimity, perhaps because she'd so recently escaped death herself, and vaguely thought she owed me a favour. 'Forget it,' she said. 'After that fright she had, Lucia doesn't remember she ever had a beast. Let's not agitate her. Children are forgetful.' They were, I knew this. She would forget all her unhappiness.

'How did the beast die?' my cousin asked.

I hesitantly described what happened.

'That's not right!' she yelled, slapping her thigh. 'The manual was very clear. Even if you forget to feed it or feed it the wrong thing, the beast shouldn't die. And not in such a strange way! They must have sold us an inferior product. I'm going to complain.' She was twisting like a fish on dry land. That was my cousin, a demon in human form.

She dragged me back to Heavenly Beauty Mall, and machine-gunned the salesgirl with questions. The poor woman nearly fainted from the onslaught. When she finally worked out what was going on, she rallied. 'Madam, you must be mistaken. We've been selling heartsick beasts for more than twenty years, and nothing like this has ever happened. No one's ever managed to kill a heartsick beast.' She glared at me, the murderer.

My cousin wouldn't give up. 'This must be your fault! I'm going to get the Consumers' Association to sue you! You can't just brush this off – these things are too expensive!'

The salesgirl scurried away to fetch her boss, whom I recognised at once as the little manager I'd met with Zhong Liang. He must have assumed I was Zhong Liang's girlfriend, because he gaped at me like his soul was leaving his body. He bowed and scraped, and before we'd said a word, he was frantically babbling, 'Sorry, so sorry, we were in the wrong. We'll compensate you for your loss, every last cent. You'll get a full refund plus twenty-five percent. I'll arrange that right away!'

Even someone as grasping as my cousin could tell this was too much. 'No need,' she said. 'A full refund will do.'

'That's not enough,' he insisted, and ushered her into his office so he could write a cheque. I followed them in. My cousin seemed perplexed, but refused to let up. She was muttering, 'It's not just about the money. The beast was made in my cousin's likeness. We didn't grow up together. I don't even have a photo of her as a little girl.'

'That's no problem,' said the manager. 'We'll just get our computer to take a picture of her, and it will tell us what she looked like when she was one, two, three, any age you like.'

And with that, he shoved me back into the imaging studio. A second later, the machinery spat out a picture. 'Look,' he said, waving it in front of me. 'That's you when you were five, or maybe a bit older. I'll make a copy for your cousin to take home.'

I looked down at the little girl. Her eyes were large and black, her skin very pale. What a sweetheart. 'Is that me?' My voice was shaking.

'Of course it is!' he said vehemently. 'This software was designed by the great man himself, the one who invented the heartsick beasts!' My professor. His fingerprints were everywhere. Ice ran through my hands, and my lips trembled.

I ripped up the photograph with unsteady hands.

'No need to make a copy,' I said. 'My cousin wasn't serious, she doesn't need to see this. And I want you to delete all my data, if that's possible.'

The little manager could tell I was upset, and agreed to do so right away. As he ushered me out, he said, 'I hope you and Mr Zhong will visit again soon!'

My cousin was beaming at her cheque. When I came back out, she grabbed me and started walking away. 'What's up with them today? Anyway, let's leave before they change their minds.'

Outside, the sun was blazing. I shut my eyes and took a deep breath. I could still see that little girl's face clearly. She was so familiar. Every New Year, while everyone else was out playing, my mum and I would sit with the nuns in the Temple of the Antiquities, glued to the TV watching that old clip of the very first heartsick beast being born. On-screen, my professor was still young, his face handsome and confident. He smiled tenderly at the little girl in his arms, and kissed her on the cheek. My mother would stroke my hand and say, 'Will you fall in love with a man like that?'

And I would smile, looking at him. 'I will.'

The little beast in his arms was so happy. I never forgot her little face, year after year. It was just appearing, like a polaroid. 'This is you as a child,' the manager had said.

I laughed and laughed.

My professor would have held me in his arms and announced to the whole world, 'This is my heartsick beast.'

He held me, but gave the patent to the government. All the heartsick beasts were killed.

Was all of this real? And if it was, was everything I knew false?

The busy city was full of people, and I passed countless strangers every day. Each of us thought the other was a lunatic. We didn't know the other's story. Anyone who knew it was dead.

I looked at my professor. 'You're my one and only treasure,' he said. 'I feel happy whenever I look at you.'

Did you ever speak these words?

He vanished before I could ask him.

—

According to the legends, there were heartsick beasts in ancient times too. When their masters passed away, they ran head first into a wall and died. Today there may be masters of knowledge who have invented heartsick beasts, but these beasts are not truly heartsick – rather, they were manufactured to serve humans.

They are domesticated, and are pure of heart – loyal and loving. Their flesh is designed to be poisonous, but only to their owners, who go mad if they taste it. The ruling class peddled heartsick beasts to common people, and after they matured at the age of five, slaughtered them for food. A portion of the flesh was tinned and delivered back to their owners who, upon eating the beast meat, lost their wits. These mindless beings were unswervingly loyal, putting their king before all else, demonstrating an unquestioning devotion that would never be overturned.

The deaths of these beasts gain the ruler his kingdom, and the masters of knowledge preserve the beast by offering it to the king. Each wins something, and continues living in peace.

The ruler wins over his people, but only when they have lost their minds. The beasts dull their owners' brains, and so lose them forever.

Is this gaining or losing? No one can say.

PRIME BEASTS

Prime beasts do not live in herds, but are dispersed through every corner of Yong'an. They love to sing, and will dance when they hear music. Their skin is coarse and mottled black, and they have a raw-boned height to them. The males have long hair, while the females keep theirs short, and wear decorative wigs. Male beasts will not permit their hair to be cut, apart from in a ritual ceremony once every three years. Any other occasion would be no different to having their heads chopped off.

Prime beasts have high noses and deep-set eyes, and gills shaped like bamboo leaves on their neck. Their lips are purplish, their hair reddish, and on their backs are breathing holes in the shape of crescent moons, about an inch long and covered by translucent red skin, just a little too opaque to see into their bodies. Other than that, they resemble humans. They are solitary by nature, and seldom speak.

These beasts rarely interact with outsiders, and even within their own tribe, the scattered members only gather once every three years, in order to propagate the species. They are short-lived, and most die soon after reaching maturity.

Legend has it that prime beasts are the descendants of executed criminals in ancient times, hence their arduous lives in Yong'an. Many are secondary school dropouts. The present local government has created an apprenticeship scheme to get them into work. Being sturdily built, many end up as security guards, and so you often see the looming figure of a prime beast outside the city's housing developments, office buildings, and nightspots.

Silently, diligently, these beasts keep Yong'an safe. From time to time, our local newspapers publish articles thanking these loyal companions for their service. And over time, having a prime beast security guard has become a status symbol; no luxury apartment building would dream of being without one.

Research shows that every Yong'an resident has seen a prime beast at least once in their lives. These are the city's best-known beasts, lauded for their uncomplaining, hard-working natures. They have earned the respect of human beings.

Prime beasts are fecund creatures, and the females

frequently produce litters of five or more. Due to their short lifespans, however, this has not increased the population; and their numbers have remained constant over the years.

As for the story about a human woman who married a prime beast, hardly anyone knows about that.

—

'You're writing another love story? Why?' Zhong Liang asked distractedly. He was slumped on my sofa, laptop on his knees, and apparently in a devilish mood.

I was still in bed, and didn't have the energy to do more than roll my eyes at him. 'Could you please be nice to me? Look at the state I'm in.'

Zhong Liang put down the computer and walked over, the better to scold me. 'You idiot. If you're going to get drunk, at least take a taxi. If you insist on walking, stick to the main roads. If you take a short-cut through the backstreets and get mugged, just hand over your bag. But no, you had to fight back, and now look at you.' He lifted my right arm, where I'd been stabbed. 'Does it still hurt?'

'It's a bloody mess. Could you not manhandle it?'

'Oh, now you're getting feisty?' He glared at me. 'Who did you call for help last night? Who drove for miles to come get you, and who brought you to the hospital to get stitches, so you wouldn't be a burden on society?'

He had a point, so I changed the subject. 'Hurry up and type, or you'll miss my deadline.'

'No good deed goes unpunished, it seems,' he grumbled. 'So I helped you, and now I have to be your scribe? Your boss really is a Scrooge.'

He sat back on the sofa, sighing. Despite everything else he was juggling, he was still able to duck the pillow I threw at him. He picked up the laptop and tried to look like a great literary figure. 'All right, go on, what's the next line?'

'Are you hungry?' asked the girl.

'No,' the beast answered. 'Just a little sleepy.'

The dark sky loomed before them – this was many years ago, before our new local government got elected, and the city was poorly maintained. Marauding groups of prime beasts lurked at every street corner, collecting protection money from passers-by and getting into fights. Meanwhile, the factories pumped sticky black smoke into the air, and the workers had to drink fizzy pop because the water was polluted too.

And now this prime beast leaned against the door frame, head hanging as he yawned. 'I'm just a little sleepy,' he repeated.

'Don't bluff,' said the girl. 'You must be hungry. How about this? I'll make you a bowl of dumplings.'

The beast looked her in the eye and said, coldly, 'Don't try to trick me. Come on, hand over your protection money.' His hair was very long, and pulled up into a bun. His dark skin gleamed in the sunlight, making him look like an enormous boulder. Watching him from behind her counter, the girl couldn't help giggling.

This angered the beast. 'What's so funny?' he growled.

She told him he looked like a boulder, and that made him laugh too.

This beast had fled a long way before coming back to this city. Everything felt strange to him, and he actually hadn't heard of this thing called protection money before. After moving back into his home, he cleared out the rubbish and sat in his empty room, wondering what to do next. He phoned the Prime Beast Association, and someone told him to collect protection money, so here he was. As for how to do this, or even how much to collect, he had no idea. Was he meant to beat up this young woman?

Here's what happened that first day: he woke up, and once his eyes had adjusted to the glaring daylight, he walked down that long street, following the strong whiff of dried chillies to the provision store. This was a smallish establishment, just a wooden board for a counter, upon which were displayed a jumble of star anise, cinnamon, Sichuan peppercorns, ginger, sesame oil, soy sauce, and other hotpot ingredients. The girl sat behind the counter scraping lazily at a large block of brown sugar, occasionally licking the spoon.

He watched her for a while before entering the shop. She'd just tipped a full spoon of sugar into her mouth, and beamed at him – she wasn't beautiful, but there was something sweet about her smile – and he froze. She stood up. 'How can I help you?'

He cleared his throat. 'I'm here to collect protection money.'

'What money?'

'Protection money.' He sounded embarrassed.

'Sorry, what?'

'Protection money,' he said again, with some hesitation.

'What are you protecting?' She raised her head and smiled at him.

Finally, he realised she was toying with him. A little angry, he came closer and made his face look stern. 'Protection money!'

He was a fully-grown beast, and therefore both tall and broad. Like anyone far from home would be, his face was full of suffering. His nose was very straight, with shadows like mountain ridges along his face. In his eyes burned a raging fire.

The girl was unmoved, and tilted her head to one side while she considered him for a moment. 'You want to protect me?'

This caught him off guard. Before he could reply, she went on, 'But I'm in no danger at all.'

How could he manufacture some danger to make her feel in need of protection? The beast wrestled with this question all night, and finally decided that the next day, he would sit on her doorstep, and whenever a customer approached, he would block the entrance with his legs, twisting around to say to the girl, 'Protection money.'

It wasn't a bad plan, but as it turned out, business at the provision shop wasn't that great. He stayed there till three o'clock, and not a single customer showed up. The beast leaned against the door frame, listening to the girl's spoon scraping the block of sugar. He almost fell asleep several times. Then the girl had asked, 'Are you hungry?'

All of a sudden, he was ravenous, but he answered, 'No, just a little sleepy.'

Nonetheless, she insisted on making him a bowl of sweet soup with twenty dumplings in it, some filled with brown sugar and sesame paste, others with chopped peanuts.

The beast devoured them with gusto.

'Tasty?' asked the girl, then without waiting for an answer, she murmured as if to herself, smiling, 'Girls eat these dumplings when they're about to get married. It's very auspicious.' She smiled, her unbeautiful features lighting up.

He almost choked.

'I think I'm falling in love with you,' he said abruptly.

'Hang on!' Zhong Liang cried out. 'I can't stand this any more. Why do you make all your male characters so ridiculous? Also, haven't you ever gone out with anyone? Since when do things move so fast?'

'Who's the author, you or me?' My eyes remained glued on the TV show I was watching, and I sipped at a glass of milk. 'First of all, that's how you tell a story. And secondly, I only get three thousand words per issue. I need to move fast.'

He had nothing to say to that, poor boy. Finally, he muttered, 'No matter how I look at it, I always feel like you're exploiting me somehow.'

I finished my milk, pressed pause, and turned my attention to him. 'Dear boy, you saw how badly injured I was last night. Twelve stitches in my right hand! You think I'm faking it?'

He was silent for a second. 'Did you get a close look at the guy? If you can give me a rough description, I promise I'll drag him out from whatever rock he's hiding under—'

'Thrash him to within an inch of his life, and hang him from the city gate?' I interrupted, shaking my head. 'My dear young master Zhong, I'm afraid your strongman services won't be required in this matter. I didn't see his face. Anyway, sometimes a loss of money can be auspicious. It prevents disaster.'

Zhong Liang snorted. 'You lost money, sure, but disaster came anyway. That bastard really roughed you up. When I saw you yesterday, I thought someone had done a hit job on you. You were covered in injuries...' He slapped a hand across his mouth, turned to look at me, and after some hesitation, finally said, 'I'm sorry, I didn't mean to mention it again.'

'It's fine.' I had to smile at how guilty he looked. 'I'll spare you the death penalty, but you still have to be punished. Go to the kitchen and cook me fifteen dumplings. Five peanut, five brown sugar, and five sesame. Not one less!'

Zhong Liang sparked back to life. 'You've been eating solidly for three hours now, you pig! So you got mugged – you don't get to sit around gorging yourself! Don't give up on yourself just because you're a spinster.' But he was already heading into the kitchen.

'I think I'm falling in love with you,' he said abruptly.

'Boil the dumplings till they're soft,' I yelled after him.

'You think what?' said the girl. She often seemed distracted and didn't hear things, as if her mind was perpetually on another planet.

'Nothing,' said the beast hastily, his heart jumping like crazy. 'So when can you pay the protection money?'

'How much is it?' she finally asked.

'I honestly hadn't thought of that.' He turned it over in his mind for a full five minutes. 'How about fifty?'

'Fifty?' she exclaimed.

'Yes, fifty.' His voice was uncertain.

'So cheap? If I give you fifty, will you really protect me forever?' The beast felt dizzy. What an alarming situation, a thug collecting protection money for the first time, encountering a small business owner who'd never paid it before. 'Where did you live before this?' he couldn't help asking.

'I was at school, but then there was some family trouble, so I came out here to look after the shop,' she explained. Then as if she couldn't help going back to the subject, 'Really, you'll protect me for just fifty? And you'll help me change the gas cylinder?'

'No, I meant fifty a month,' said the beast.

'Well, then that's too expensive,' she pouted.

'What do you think is fair?'

'How about twenty?'

'Twenty-five.'

'All right,' she said, 'But you have to help me change the gas.'

'Fine.'

She rummaged in her bag and found a hundred yuan bill, which she handed to the prime beast.

'Don't you have anything smaller?' said the beast, a little shamefaced. 'I don't have any change.'

She looked again and found some coins. 'I have 23.50.'

The beast forced a smile and took the cash. 'That's okay, call it an introductory discount.'

'Great!' She grinned and ate another spoonful of brown sugar.

Her smile was so beautiful, the beast felt unsteady

on his feet. The thought went through his mind: had she short-changed him on purpose?

Before he could ponder the question more fully, the beast found himself being sent out with the girl for a new gas cylinder, two streets away. Between the rain and the roadworks, they were practically wading through mud. There were slogans painted in black ink on the telegraph poles. The prime beast was very tall, and walked in front with the cylinder on his shoulder, while the young woman followed behind, skipping between puddles. After a while, she got bored and walked beside the beast, studying him intently. 'What's that on your neck?' she asked abruptly.

'Gills,' said the beast.

Many years ago, he'd glided silently through the Lotus River, away from Yong'an City. He'd only just been born, but already, he knew how to breathe. The icy water passed through the gills in his neck and into his body. Having left his mother's body, he experienced cold for the first time. There were five of them, five children, like tiny, feeble fish. They left the city along with the plastic bags, fallen leaves and beer bottles in the water, but even at such a young age, he knew he would be back.

'Why did you leave? And why did you come

back?' asked the girl casually, as she stood behind the counter rearranging new stock.

He didn't know how to answer her. She was a human woman, different from him, with her pale skin, fine bones and flat Chinese face that only grew animated when she smiled. Just as he had that thought, she smiled again, and walked over to touch his knotted hair. 'Why?' she asked.

And that's when he kissed her.

'What's wrong?' said Zhong Liang. He put down the laptop and came over to touch my forehead. 'What is it? Are you in pain? Why are you crying?'

I looked up at his face, which was lowered and in beautiful shadow. 'What is it?' he said again. The night before, I'd phoned him because there was no one else in this vast city that I could ask. 'Zhong Liang,' I'd said, 'Come over, quick, I've been mugged.' He was there in five minutes, standing in front of me just as he was now, head hung, and asking, 'What is it? What's wrong?'

I'd looked at him and burst into loud sobs.

I wanted to be as innocent as him, as clear and unruffled. If only I could ask my professor and my mother, *what is it, what's wrong?*

I couldn't say the words, and neither of them

would be able to answer me in any case.

Through a combination of threats and promises, I'd inveigled my editor into using his contacts to put me in touch with an elderly prime beast, apparently one with a high standing in his community. Few prime beasts ever reached his age – and he knew several generations' worth of stories. He had a pension of 1,000 yuan a month, and lived in a residential care home where he kept a hwamei bird. His existence was circumscribed, but fairly happy.

He came to visit one day. He sat across from me, just the two of us. I regarded him cautiously. He was still strapping, with an aquiline nose and the genetically encoded good looks of a beast, warm as a sunny afternoon. I felt compelled to speak first. 'Have you heard anything about a prime beast marrying a human woman?'

He looked at me as if I hadn't spoken. Only his gills fluttered lightly in the breeze.

I repeated the question.

'I don't know anything about that,' he said.

Growing agitated, I grasped his hand and blurted, 'I know this may be a secret you beasts keep among yourself, but please tell me!' After a moment, I added quietly, 'I'm their child. I have a red crescent moon mark on my back, the sign of mixing.'

Startled, he gripped my hand and looked into my eyes. 'What did you say?' His voice shook.

'I'm their child,' I said again, choking. 'My mother told me my father was a prime beast, but I couldn't tell anyone. No one would have anything to do with me if they knew. She made me promise not to ever meet a prime beast, not a single one. I promised, and now I'm betraying her, just as she betrayed me by dying.'

The old beast stared at me for a very long time, then he laughed. 'You're lying.'

'I'm not, I can show you my birthmark. I don't have gills, but I do have the mark—'

'No,' he interrupted. 'Go now. I don't want to see you again.'

Was I lying, or was he? No one could say.

Did my mother lie to me, or did my professor? I had no way of knowing. The dead are separated from the living. If the child in this story wasn't me, then who was it? Where was she now?

I needed answers. I had to ask every person who could possibly separate the truth from the myths for me.

'What's this about?' Zhong Liang sat down, hugging me and stroking my back, comforting me like my professor used to do. 'Don't cry, don't cry.' His voice went husky. 'I'm here, aren't I? No matter what, I'm here. Shh...'

'Show some respect for your elders,' I muttered as he patted my head energetically. 'You're knocking out all my sense,' I said.

'Be quiet,' he said sternly, then folded me into a vehement embrace.

'Can I be with you?' said the beast. 'Can I?'

She looked at him for a while. 'Will you help me change the gas cylinder?'

'I will.'

'And you'll stop charging me protection money?'

'That's right.'

'Then yes.' She grinned.

The beast decided to stop collecting protection money altogether. He packed his small bag and moved into the provision shop. There was a little room behind the shop, then an airwell, and finally a kitchen. With the new gas cylinder they'd fetched that afternoon, they cooked dinner, then sat in the airwell to eat it. The girl said, 'Do you beasts often get together with humans?'

He was silent for some time. 'I don't think so,' he eventually said.

'Then why are you with me?'

'Because…' He paused to think about it. 'Because your smile is so delightful.'

She tried hard to hold back her laugh, but it broke out anyway. 'You're lying,' she said.

'It's true.'

It was true. Even much later, years after the beast had vanished from her and everyone else's lives, she never doubted that he'd loved her. There was no reason for this, no logic. The moment he'd laid eyes on her, he'd fallen in love.

The following month was the prime beast match-making ceremony that took place once every three years, but he couldn't wait for that, nor for the female beast looking forward to his return – she'd surely have on an enormous wig, which blocked out the sun entirely. Instead, he went off the rails, and fell in love with this girl.

She was a very adorable girl. She stared into space all day long, flinging all sorts of questions at him, like, 'Why is your hair so long?'

'No reason,' said the beast. 'Many things are so just out of habit. The poor female beasts in my tribe have to shave their heads, and wear these ridiculous wigs. Just as how I suddenly fell in love with you, there's no reason for it.'

She blushed and ate more food. 'Such a glib

tongue,' she scolded him, putting a piece of braised pork on his plate.

'I'll cut it off next month,' he said.

'Does that mean you'll stop loving me next month?'

He sighed long and hard, and rapped his knuckles on her head. 'Why would you think such a thing?'

'Come to think of it, why *do* male prime beasts keep their hair so long?' asked Zhong Liang. 'I know they cut it off when they come of age, then the tribe arranges for them to mate with a female beast. Could their hair be some sort of switch to turn their desire on and off?'

He turned to look at me dubiously. 'You have long hair. Is that because you're afraid no one will marry you?'

I threw my cup at him.

He caught it nimbly, and went on, unrepentant. 'No wonder our professor kept his hair so short. His head was prickly, like a hedgehog—'

The plate caught him unawares. He yelped, and protested, 'No need for that. Can't I criticise him for once without you throwing flatware at me?'

'I'm just trying to stop you talking nonsense,' I said. 'All that time with him, and you have no academic rigour at all.'

'As if you do,' he said, quick as a flash. 'You haven't done a thing with yourself. I have no idea why he missed you for so long.'

'He missed me?' I couldn't help it, the words came to my mouth.

'Yes,' he said, not noticing my expression, eager to gossip. 'He was always mentioning you. If I so much as picked up a mug, he'd say, "That was her favourite mug." The whole lab was a shrine to you.' It took him a moment to realise this hadn't struck the right note. 'I mean, he missed you the way a dad misses his daughter when she gets married and moves out,' he said awkwardly.

My face was white. 'You think he was like a father to me? Really? The man who smiled and smacked my cheeks, and said, "You give me more headaches than any other woman on earth." That man?'

Only now did Zhong Liang notice the pain in my voice. After so many years in the lab, even he had heard the rumours floating on the wind. He tried to cover up with a joke. 'Well, you know, he was the emperor, and I'd be just the old minister sent by him to look after the bratty princess.'

'Old minister?' I sneered. 'I can still smell your mother's milk on you. You're too young to even be a stable boy.'

He lost his temper at that – I must have injured his male pride. 'You stupid woman, your moods change faster than the weather. Weren't you just crying? And now you're making fun of me for being young – but I'm only seven months and three days younger than you, you know.'

In the heat of argument, I didn't have time to be astonished that he knew my birthday. 'Oh right, I forgot,' I said, reaching for the angriest words I could muster. 'You're not a prodigy like me. They probably kept you back a year.'

'Say one more word,' he growled, 'And I'll delete every line you wrote today.'

Well. There was nothing I could say to that. 'Oh, please don't, dear grand lord Mr Zhong Liang, long may your noble life be.' I was two weeks late with this manuscript, and my editor had threatened to cut off my electricity and water if I didn't hand something in. Onwards.

The prime beast ended up going to the gathering anyway. One night, he got a phone call telling him where to go the next day. 'All right,' he said, and hung up.

The woman reached out for him drowsily from

the bed. 'Why are you still up?'

He lay down, but couldn't get to sleep. After a while, she asked, 'What's wrong?'

'If I wanted to leave this place,' he said, 'would you come with me?'

'All right,' she replied, her voice slurred. She frowned. 'Come and warm me up, I'm cold.'

Whenever she frowned, he felt as if the sky was caving in. He rolled over and embraced her small, icy body. Just like his mother before she died, in his arms, looking up at him, her entire person withering before his eyes.

They had steamed buns for breakfast. When he left, she said, 'Can't I come with you?'

'No,' he said, smiling.

She understood. Yong'an was a huge, filthy, ungovernable city, full of all sorts of beasts of unknown origin, and secrets, likewise. Everyone tacitly accepts this, and gets on with their lives.

So she sat in her provision shop. There were no customers that day, so she kept scraping at the brown sugar, spooning the stuff into her mouth, spitting out the coarser grains. She'd got through half the block when he showed up. His hair had been cut off. It was a cold day, and he had a scarf over his mouth. Puffs of white floated out of his nose. He looked like a tall, handsome human man. Without saying a word, he walked over, knelt, and hugged her tight. In a low voice, he said, 'Do you love me?'

They'd only lived together a month, they were practically strangers to each other. And yet here he was, asking her this question of a lifetime. *Do you love me.*

She stroked his back, and felt the two crescent moon breath holes. 'Will you buy me lots of brown sugar?'

'Yes.'

'Then I love you.'

'What if I can't afford it?'

'I'll still love you.'

That's the kind of girl she was, and the kind of beast he was. That's how we all are, heads raised and waiting for someone to come and hold us, and ask: do you love me?

All we need to do is put out the tiniest wish. If it's fulfilled, we love that person with all our hearts; and once that happens, even if he gives us nothing more, we'll still love him.

Three days later, the girl was alone in the shop while the beast was out getting a new gas cylinder, when a customer finally showed up. Delighted, she looked up and said, 'Can I help you?'

'Give him back to me,' said the female beast.

She was tall, with distinctive features and piercing eyes. Her wig spread from her head like a pair of wings, and her gills were flapping with agitation. Without waiting to be asked, she took a seat opposite the girl. 'You can't be with him,' she said. 'Us prime beasts can't be with humans.'

'Why not?' asked the girl.

'No reason,' said the beast patiently. 'It's just tradition. There are so few of us, we can't afford to marry outside the tribe and dilute our bloodline. We all have a mate chosen for us. He's mine.'

The girl looked at her. She was a very beautiful beast. Her neck was long, her bearing regal. There was sadness in her eyes, and her skin was dark and coarse. The girl made a decision in her head, and said, 'You should leave. We're together now.'

The beast was shocked, but tried to argue. 'You should break up. This won't end well. Us beasts are the descendants of the executed. Our lives are hard, and our traditions rock-solid. He'll leave you sooner or later.'

The girl saw how beautiful she was, and smiled. 'I don't believe that.' She pronounced those four words very slowly, using up all the strength in her body. Before the last one left her mouth, the male beast had left her.

His leaving had nothing to do with the female beast. It was because of their child.

The beast said, 'We can't allow this baby to be born. Get rid of it. We can't ever have children.'

The girl, who was now thoroughly a woman, said, 'I'm going to have my child no matter what.' She could feel its every breath. 'This is our child.'

'No,' said the beast, in agony. 'It will be a halfling.'

'A halfling?' Tears poured down her face, and she started wailing like a vulgar fishwife. 'Please, let me have my baby. I want a child, a child of my own. Our child. If you love me, why can't you love our child?'

They argued for a very long time, perhaps a week, or perhaps even longer than the time they'd been in love for. In the end, the beast said, 'All right.'

The woman had the child, but the child had no father. The prime beast left them just as suddenly as he'd arrived. The woman had to fetch her own gas cylinders now.

Then the child grew up. That's the whole story.

'That's it?' Zhong Liang stared at me in disbelief.

'Yes,' I said. 'Don't you know how valuable space is in a newspaper? If I went past my word limit, my editor would have my head.'

Zhong Liang reluctantly saved the document, and shut down the laptop. 'It must be nice to be an author,' he said, then seemed to feel he'd used the wrong word. 'I mean, a writer.'

His tone was dismissive, but I didn't care. I shut my eyes and took a deep breath, thinking about what my mother had told me. Everything she'd said about my father. These were all her words I'd just written. When she'd told me everything, she'd asked, 'Do you hate him?'

'I don't know,' I said.

My mother looked surprised. Perhaps so much time had passed that she no longer resembled the woman in the story. She'd said, 'If it were me, I would hate him. He left, just like that. I don't know if he went back to the female beast. As for the child, would she feel she was a halfling? A fatherless halfling. Neither human nor beast.' She sighed.

'No,' I said, stroking her face. The air in the Temple of the Antiquities was fragrant and calming. 'I have a good life,' I said. 'Hatred would destroy me.'

She smiled and said, 'I brought you to the temple so you would have a peaceful heart. But even if I hadn't done that, and you became a rageful child, I wouldn't have blamed you. None of this is your fault. It's just your fate, my poor child. Like I told you, the past is the past. You mustn't ever speak to a prime beast. Not a single one. You can't meet anyone who knows about your parentage. If they know, you mustn't see them.'

She'd done as she'd said. Five days later, a fire swept through the nunnery. She lay quietly within it, like when she was a young girl.

'This is all made-up,' said Zhong Liang.

'Huh?' Still sunk in my memories, I could only stare blankly at him, like an idiot.

Frowning, he handed me a Coke. 'This is all made-up. You're getting worked up for nothing – that child isn't you. You're not that old. By the time you were born, the city had piped gas – no one went around fetching gas cylinders. God knows where you were back when this was going on.'

These words startled me from my dreams.

So for all those years, my mother had been lying to me.

But why?

She wouldn't have done it frivolously – my mother didn't do things like that. Everything she said had a reason behind it. 'Don't go looking for prime beasts,' she'd said. 'You mustn't do that.'

I'd disobeyed, and now I was bruised and injured as a result.

Preoccupied, I absently rubbed my right arm, as if I could still see light glinting off the knife. We were in a dark alleyway. I'd run for my life. My attacker had a high nose and deep-set eyes. His hair was pulled up into a topknot. He was tall and well-built, and there were gills on his neck – a prime beast.

A prime beast who wanted to kill me.

I'd sprinted as fast as I could. The bright lights and hubbub of the main road weren't too far away. Quick, run. People with secrets are steeped in sin.

My professor once said, 'I'm covered in sin from head to toe. You think I'm unscrupulous, but we all have our secrets.' He looked at me, tenderness in his eyes, the outline of his face undeniably handsome. He lowered his head and murmured, 'They don't understand, but I want you to – because you're different.'

He also said, 'You're the most special person to me in this whole world.'

And then, 'I know everything about you.'

'Hey!' Once again, Zhong Liang pulled me back to reality. 'Can we go out for dinner? I'm starving, and I've been typing for ages.'

'What?' I opened my eyes wide. 'But I'm seriously injured!'

He brought his face closer, till it was almost touching mine, and grinned. 'Never mind, dear friend. I don't want to eat alone – it makes me feel lonely. I'll carry you down the stairs, and drive you to the most comfortable restaurant I can find. We'll come straight home after our meal. How about that? Do you prefer Japanese cuisine or Korean barbecue?'

I looked at him for a while, and couldn't help smiling. I wanted to hug him tight, this person who truly understood me. My professor did, and Zhong Liang did too. He wasn't being clueless, he knew about me and my fears – and what I feared most was loneliness.

'All right,' I said.

'Good girl.' He pinched my cheeks, as if he were an uncle.

I sighed. 'That's how I am, a weak-willed, foolish egghead.'

—

Zhong Liang carried me down the stairs and deposited me on the sofa in the lobby. 'Wait here,' he said gently, 'I'll go get the car from the basement.' He walked away. I grimaced at the way he'd spoken to me – as if I were an infant. Nothing to do but wait.

My flat was in an up-and-coming neighbourhood. The residents of my building were mostly young office workers, and we couldn't afford a prime beast security guard. Instead, we'd hired the tallest human male we could find. Through the glass doors, I could see a landscaped garden, and the early evening streets full of bizarrely dressed young people, and...

A prime beast.

The one from yesterday, the one in the dark alleyway.

He pushed open the door. There was no one else in the lobby. He walked up me with his imposing bulk, looking down at me like an emperor and said, 'I want you to die.'

The beast said, 'I want you to die. You know why? If I hadn't injured you yesterday, you'd probably have killed old Mr Lei by now—'

'Old Mr Lei?' I was a novelist, after all, and even at this life-threatening moment, my curiosity couldn't help rearing its eager head.

'Don't pretend you don't know,' he said impatiently. 'You may be mixed, but your life force is strong. Still, I'm going to kill you. Old Mr Lei raised me, and helped kill my parents. My gratitude to him—'

'What did you say?' I needed to catch up.

'Enough nonsense!' The beast pulled out his dagger and thrust it at me. 'You have prime beast blood in you, you ought to know this is your destiny.'

My destiny. The lobby was starkly empty. Who knew where our lackadaisical security guard had sloped off to? I shut my eyes and waited to die.

'What the hell?' Zhong Liang's voice. He'd caught hold of the knife, and I heard a shearing sound from the beast's wrist – probably dislocated. Very good, Zhong Liang. Of course, the son of a rich man would be trained in several martial arts.

'Stop that!' Like a sparrow swooping down on a praying mantis just as it nabbed a cicada, who should come striding through the glass doors now but an older prime beast. Zhong Liang froze, and so did I. My life was getting more dramatic by the moment.

The old beast – old Mr Lei, I presumed – came closer and growled, 'Stop,' again, at Zhong Liang. Then, as if no one else was around, he said to the younger beast, 'What do you think you're doing?'

Sweat was beading on the young beast's brow. 'Godfather,' he muttered.

Godfather? If not for the dire circumstances, I would have burst out laughing. A revered leader, no less. This sort of thing didn't even happen in wuxia novels. I could understand why prime beasts would operate this way – being the descendants of criminals, they lived an outlaw existence.

'Godfather,' said the young beast, 'She was trying to find out about you. She's your child, which means she'll kill you sooner or later. I knew you wouldn't do anything about it, so I wanted to strike first.'

Zhong Liang and I stared at him, and I thought, 'So I actually managed to track down the main character in my story with my first guess – but he wouldn't be this old, would he?'

The old beast laughed and, without even glancing at Zhong Liang, snapped the young beast's wrist back into place and patted him on the shoulder. 'Silly boy. Even if this were my child with a human woman, I'd be the only one who could kill her. Anyway, she's not. I don't know why she knows so much, but she's far too young, and our child was a boy.'

The young beast's face turned ashen, while Zhong Liang looked baffled. Ignoring their reactions, the old beast took the young one by the hand and said, 'Come on, let's go home. We'll be fine. We're prime beasts, we have our own destinies – let's not worry about other people's.'

Just like that, the shadow of death was gone. The young prime beast meekly allowed himself to be led away. The old one turned back to glance at me, a thousand words in his eyes, but not one of them passing his lips.

As for me, I remained on the sofa, my body full of pain and my mouth quivering, as if I wanted to call someone's name – but I didn't make a sound. Whose name? My mother's, or my professor's? They'd understood me, but they'd both lied to me.

'Don't go looking for the prime beast,' my mother had said. 'Whatever happens, don't go.' So many layers of meaning in those words. And here's how things had turned out.

She told me the story of the prime beast the same way my professor told it to her. She told me I was the child in the story, and added, 'If you'd turned out stubborn, I wouldn't have blamed you. My poor child.' Those were the words she probably didn't say to him back then.

There is so much we don't understand, and no one can escape their fate. My professor, the dashingly famous and cruel star of Yong'an University, walked into the lecture theatre on that first day, and saw a roomful of brand-new students. When he took attendance, the third name was mine. He broke into a cold sweat, and looked up to see my face. My face, as we know, was almost identical to my mother's.

I was thin-skinned, and couldn't shrug off the way he called my name again and again, making me answer each time. I'd stormed out, and he roared after me, 'If you have the guts, don't ever come back!' When my mother left him, he must have been even angrier. He smashed every item in his lab and screamed, "If you have the guts, don't ever come back! Take the baby with you! Don't you dare come back!'

But I came back.

When you saw me again, I no longer understood you.

That was our story. So close, and yet so far away.

Everything blurred before my eyes, but I dug my nails into my palm, until they left deep marks in the flesh, and almost drew blood. Still I hadn't made a sound.

Zhong Liang recovered first. 'Was that some kind of performance art?'

I had to laugh – that there were people in the world with such simple minds. He would surely live to be a hundred.

He came over and lifted me to my feet. 'Let's go. I'll carry you to the car, and we'll go for dinner. Let's have a nourishing meal. And afterwards, everything will be fine.'

I looked at his face. So young, so handsome. He didn't know anything, but seemed to understand everything. He didn't ask any questions, just held me tight. 'Everything will be fine,' he said again.

Everything would be fine.

—

A week later, I got a call from an unknown number. A young male voice, choked, said, 'He's dead. He must have been killed by *him*.'

I knew who he meant. The prime beast my mother told me about so many times, the maiden's tender lover, the child's cruel father. He'd lived too long. The maiden he'd loved and who'd loved him back, the child they'd had – both dead. And now, finally, he was dead too.

That day was exactly seven weeks after my professor's death. According to the old ways, that's when mourning ends. Even tiny children know this: after forty-nine days, the soul departs for good, and is forever separated from this realm.

———

Prime beasts mostly die young. They are the descendants of condemned criminals, and have meagre destinies. Though scattered, they have held on to their shared rituals. The males wear their hair long, the females short. For thousands of years they have mated only within their own tribe.

Prime beasts have gills, and can breathe in water. They have air holes on their backs, allowing them to survive under the earth. Both characteristics were adapted by their painful lives in captivity.

Because of their harsh existences, prime beasts are strong and hardy, so they can only be hurt by their own kind. In prison, mothers would kill their children, to save them from growing up behind bars. Eventually this became their way of life – females would destroy their young. Perhaps one in six would survive, and when these were grown, they would slaughter their own parents and feast on their flesh.

For thousands of years, this has been the nature of prime beasts. This has been their fate. A lonely, strong tribe, fine-boned and good-looking, taking pleasure in song and dance, indestructible.

The long-lived amongst them are lawless, while the short-lived are noble as their days wane. This is the way of their world.

RETURNING BEASTS

The returning beasts stay hidden during the day and only appear at night – and as a result, are rarely seen. If you are fated not to encounter them, you never will, no matter how hard you try. Yet if your destinies are linked, then you will come together no matter what. They are the descendants of ancient tomb robbers. After the last ancient grave had been dug up and plundered, they came to Yong'an.

These beasts are small and feeble. Their red eyes can see in the dark, and their fingers are long and slender. Their feet are flat, and their soles, like the palms of their hands, are thick with fur, allowing them to move soundlessly. They have small ears and don't like to talk – most of them stutter. Their extremely pale skin is blinding in daylight, and faintly luminous at night. Other than these things, they are no different from human beings.

Returning beasts like quiet. They enjoy herbal

jelly and glutinous rice congee, and loathe smoked meat and tofu. Their hobbies include building walls – that is, walls of mahjong tiles at the gambling table.

Beneath Yong'an is a City of the Dead, which the returning beasts build and maintain. Most of the time they are hard at work underground, only emerging after dark to scurry home and sleep. They are the only creatures in Yong'an who know the whereabouts of the deceased.

For reasons unknown, there are individuals who roam the earth and stake their fortunes on being able to see the dead one more time – but whether any have had their wishes realised, no one can say.

There is an ancient saying: birth is a process of returning, death is a process of longing. The returning beasts serve the dead, but perhaps this is the origin of their name.

—

It was the winter break, but Yong'an University campus was still full of people. The lotuses in the pond had shed their leaves, and all around everyone was talking about days gone by. Entering by the western gate, you'd walk around the lotus pond, down the avenue littered with pagoda tree leaves, then turn left and take the first right – and you'd see an enormous eucalyptus tree, the sort that covers plains, its vast, tangled crown green in all seasons, endlessly shedding leaves and casting a broad shadow. The small building that housed the zoology labs lay entirely within its shade.

My professor often stood at the window, gazing at the eucalyptus tree, smoking one cigarette after another. Once when I'd asked him what he was thinking, he said, 'From a certain angle, the crown of that tree looks like a mystic symbol.'

It was summer when I first arrived here. The other girls on campus had such snowy white skin, it dazzled me. I told my professor this, and he laughed. 'That means nothing. Not one of them is innocent.'

I didn't understand what he was saying, and he explained, 'Don't you see? All of us humans are corrupted and foolish. Our veins flow with sullied blood.' He looked a little hysterical. All of a sudden, he reached out to touch my face and smiled. 'Better if you never understand.'

A story from a long time ago.

Now I pushed the door open – it creaked with old age – and went in. There he was, his back to me. Taller than most southerners, hair very short, looking cosy in his thick padded jacket. He was smoking as he gazed into the distance, although the thin layer of frost covering the window made it impossible to see out.

I took a deep breath. The air was icy-cold. Voice trembling, I said, 'You're back?'

He froze for a moment, stubbed out his cigarette on the sill, and turned to smile at me. 'You've come back too, haven't you?' It was Zhong Liang.

Zhong Liang's boyish smile lit up his radiant face, and seemed to drive the gloom from the room. He sprang towards me, rather like a frog. 'What are you doing here?'

I had nothing to say.

Luckily, the boy wonder didn't wait for a response. 'Ah! I suppose you missed me. I'm just a lonely little scientist, doing my meaningless experiments.'

'Scientists are the purest artists. Their craft is directed at drawing closer to the infinite void.' Something my professor once said.

'Are you an artist, then?' I'd retorted, laughing.

'What do you want for dinner?' Zhong Liang asked.

'Huh?' I came back to myself. 'Oh, anything.'

'Well said,' he replied. 'It doesn't matter what you eat, the important thing is who you're eating with.'

I rolled my eyes at him, trying to squash his habitual self-regard. 'It's late, shall we just go for a drink?' I said, keeping my voice frosty.

'Sure, sure.' He was far too useless to ever say no to me.

—

The Dolphin Bar was unusually empty. It was a few days to the New Year, and everyone must have been home enjoying family togetherness. The first time I came here, I was drawn by the giant neon-blue dolphin, flickering like the start of a porno. I went in, but there was no pleasure to be had here. It was just a little pub, with a taciturn barman who never bothered the single women patrons, but silently poured them drink after drink. If you had one too many, all you had to do was head for the cherry-red bathroom and make yourself vomit.

Zhong Liang and I sat at the bar, while the bartender stood at the other end chuckling at the TV. Just the three of us, a pitiful sight. After two drinks, I murmured to Zhong Liang, 'I feel like I'm going to die soon.'

He laughed.

In bars like this, on nights like this, the people of Yong'an would talk of death. Death began sprouting in every baby's body, and took a human lifetime to reach maturity. By the time it flowered, all its energy was spent. I drank some more, and said slowly, again, with a great deal of effort, 'I feel like I'm about to die.'

Everything I'd lived and loved was now fixed in place. I'd used the life I had to understand his story, her story, their story. Now I knew it all, I had no story of my own.

And now it was time for the curtain to fall.

I clinked glasses with Zhong Liang. The bar faced the main door, which stood ajar. I shivered from the cold wind rushing in. Zhong Liang touched my hand, frowned at its iciness, and got up to shut the door.

I watched him from behind. In the dim light, his back looked sad, just like my professor's. It felt as if he were walking away, and I would never see him again.

'Zhong Liang,' I cried out, my voice strangely quiet.

He didn't hear me. As he reached out for the door, another customer came in, brushing past him.

This person only came up to Zhong Liang's shoulder. His head was down, and he walked in without a word, muffled up in a thick coat, woollen hat and long scarf.

The newcomer strode up to the bar and stepped on a stool to clamber into the high chair. He rapped the counter and called, 'Service!' His voice was hoarse and unpleasant. Zhong Liang came back to his seat, brows crinkled. 'Probably a busker,' he whispered to me.

I laughed to myself. Zhong Liang's sense of humour was incurably dry.

Yet the barman, spoiled by years of exposure to the clientele, was even drier. The little bastard all but pressed his entire face against the glass and said, 'Just a moment.'

I couldn't stop the laughter escaping. The newcomer turned and glanced at me.

Just one look.

He was odd-looking – an almost flat face, extremely pasty skin, so pale it glowed in the gloom. His eyes were reddish. He stared straight at me.

I pulled back, and a shiver went through me.

Zhong Liang noticed. 'Still cold?' He draped his jacket across my shoulders.

I didn't hear him. The stranger held all my attention. He'd already turned back, and was peering over the counter like a soldier in a siege, his long fingers rhythmically tap, tap, tapping.

The bartender finally came over. 'What are you having?'

The stranger grabbed the barman's wrist. 'Come with me.'

Startled, the barman tried to pull away, but couldn't

free himself. 'You – what do you think you're doing?'

'Come with me!' The man's voice was coarse and raspy, filing away at my nerves.

'Come where? I don't fucking know you! Fucking hell, you nutjob—' The bartender might have been a man of few words, but most of them were four-letter ones – he was a man of the world.

Zhong Liang realised something was wrong and tugged at me to leave, but I was frozen, as if I'd been nailed to my seat, eyes fixed on the pair.

Scared now, Zhong Liang tried to drag me to my feet, leaning over to say, 'There's going to be a fight! We need to get out of here!'

Sure enough, the barman smashed the bottom of a bottle, ready to launch it at the stranger's head.

Instead, it came down on the counter.

The stranger let go and ducked aside, looking confused. He glanced at the barman. 'This isn't right,' he said. 'This isn't right.'

His head spun round, and he caught sight of me and Zhong Liang. 'Did I get it wrong?' he muttered to himself.

I recovered my senses and jumped to my feet, startling Zhong Liang. I walked over to the man and said, 'Hi—'

He seemed terrified. Without even meeting my

eye, he tumbled out of his chair and was through the door in a flash.

It took me a second to recover and run after him. Cold air smashed me in the face. The streets were full of cars, but there was not a soul in sight.

Zhong Liang came sprinting after me. 'What do you think you're doing? You don't need to pull a stunt like this just to get out of paying your bar tab.' He handed me my coat.

I stood blankly. When I turned to him, my face was covered in tears.

'What is it? What happened?' Zhong Liang, the bookworm, was at a loss.

I produced four incoherent syllables.

'What's that?' He bent his ear to my mouth.

'Returning beast,' I said.

Could you bring me to see the dead? The soul of my professor. I have so much I still want to ask him.

Could you?

Without warning, Zhong Liang chose this moment let his scientist-self erupt. As if shocked by electricity, he grabbed me and started running.

'Where are we going?' I asked, perplexed, tears still wet on my face.

'That's a rare specimen! After him!' He was exhilarated, never mind that this supernatural creature was probably miles away by now. That was Zhong Liang to the core, operating on instinct rather than intellect. When he set out on a course of action, there was no stopping him.

He was very fast, like a long-legged runner in a fairy tale. As I dragged behind him, he combed the vast, noisy city for this unknown returning beast. How he longed to track him down. Even though he must have known there was no hope, he understood how much it would mean to me.

At the next junction, we turned into a little road. It was late enough that there was no one around. Panting hard, I gasped, 'Stop, stop, I can't.'

'No!' His face wasn't red, and he wasn't even breathing hard. 'I need to find him. I'm a scientist!'

I would have kicked the idiot, but he'd abruptly stopped. I stumbled ahead, but he quickly pulled me back.

The beast was by the side of the road.

He was lying on his side. His hat had fallen off, revealing his brittle hair and unattractive face. A knife stuck out of his chest, exactly where his heart would be – so accurately placed, a surgeon could have done it.

Before I could make sense of what I was seeing, I heard Zhong Liang shout, 'Hey, you! Stop running!'

I followed his gaze and saw a figure swiftly disappearing around the corner.

Zhong Liang gave chase, but he'd only taken a couple of steps when I called his name.

He turned to see me on my knees, vigorously throwing up. A chill wind filled my guts, while food and beer rushed out of me. It felt like I was spewing from every orifice, mouth and nose, eyes and ears. What a mess.

'Zhong Liang...' I moaned.

He came to me and gently stroked my back. 'I see you had an omelette for lunch,' he said blandly.

When I die, it will probably be from rage at this man.

———

The Zhong family was wealthy and powerful enough that they could block out the sky by raising a single hand. When I looked at reports of the murder the next day, they called it a mugging gone tragically wrong, blaming thugs from the countryside. There was a blurry picture, countless comments, and that was that. The puddle of vomit I'd left at the scene had mysteriously vanished.

I looked up from the newspapers to see Zhong Liang walking towards me with a glass of water. I took a sip – the perfect temperature, neither too hot nor too cold. He'd have made an excellent maid. I drank while he sat across from me, frowning.

'What is it?' I asked. He was making me nervous.

He didn't answer, but the folds in his brow could have trapped a fly. He walked over absently, put a hand to my forehead, and sighed. 'When will you stop worrying me? You were talking in your sleep all night, and that high fever – at least you're better now.'

'What did I say?' I felt a moment of panic.

Zhong Liang stared at me with an expression I'd never seen him wear before. His face was handsome and open as ever, but there was such darkness in his eyes that I couldn't look directly at them. I opened my mouth, but couldn't recall what I'd been about to say. He lowered his head, drew closer, and said, 'Is there anything you don't want me to find out?'

'No,' I said, like a condemned criminal.

He was silent for a moment, then finally stepped back. I let out a long breath. Like a magic trick, his face had reverted to its usual sunny, slappable shape. 'I know everything, anyway,' he said smugly.

'Yes, yes, you do,' I laughed.

The flowers on the path, young gentleman, the blossoms on the peach tree branch, the warbling orioles – you see my fragrant front, my charming smile, but how could you know my weeping in the night, my shadowy dreams?

When the beast died so abruptly the night before, I'd been first shocked, then relieved. Now I wouldn't be able to see my professor after all. We were both stubborn people. The day he left, I'd wanted never to see him again – and sure enough, I got my wish.

Perhaps I was afraid to see him, afraid to visit the city filled with dead people, all strangers. This was what I had come to understand. They were my father, my mother, but I was just the child they'd produced out of nothing. Why did they treat me the way they did? I wanted to find them and ask, 'Do you love me? Do you? Why did you do this to me?'

But none of that mattered any more.

I knew my life would end soon. I was an outsider in this vast city. My professor and my mother were the only ones who'd understood me, and they were gone. I would travel down the long tunnel, wading through the channel, clambering with dripping wet feet onto the first step I saw, and go looking for them in the place of the dead.

When I was very little, my mother told me about a place that every child in Yong'an heard about. 'Be good,' she said. 'Don't play in the water, or returning beasts will drag you down to the City of the Dead. It's beneath the ground, and infinitely large. You'll never find your way to the edge, or an exit. In this place, every building is grey – hospitals, schools, public offices, and all food is tasteless – ice-cream, chocolate, biscuits. If you go there, you'll never return.'

There were a lot of stories like this. Mothers would say, 'Eat your vegetables, do your homework, wash your hands before dinner, otherwise...'

Otherwise... I had to laugh.

To think the greatest catastrophe that could be imagined when I was a child, was no more than this.

Zhong Liang stayed with me all day. From time to time, he'd slip into that alarming melancholy that made me wonder if he'd been drugged. At dinner time, he bought some frozen dumplings and said, 'Let's eat here – no need to go out.'

I was strongly against this idea. 'You made me stay in bed all day, but I need some fresh air.'

He strode over and leaned his bulk intimidatingly over me. 'Do as you're told.'

'Respect your elders,' I retorted.

'Act your age,' he snapped back.

'Are you calling me old?' I leapt to my feet. He should really have known better than to prod that sore spot.

Something about my face must have scared him, because he gave in right away. 'All right, fine, we'll go out.'

—

The restaurant across the road from my building was expensive and served dreadful food – I was constantly puzzled by how it managed to stay open – but Zhong Liang insisted on going there. In an instant we'd sat down and he was ordering, looking very serious, while I sat meekly. Feeling bullied, I muttered, 'What are you so afraid of? Won't let me go out...'

Somehow, he heard that. He looked at me and said, his voice equally low, 'I'm afraid you'll vanish from my side.'

And I heard that too.

We sat in silence.

I'd already decided, as I sat quietly eating my last meal; I would go, I would leave this false world others had constructed for me, and seek my final home in the City of the Dead. Even if I couldn't find a returning beast, I could simply die. The deceased will never part, and their long days stretch forever.

'Someone's watching us,' Zhong Liang abruptly said.

'Get over yourself.' I glared at him. 'You think people are looking at you twenty-four hours a day, rain or shine.'

'I'm serious,' he insisted. 'Over there.' He pointed. 'Behind that flower planter. I'm sure.'

'Yes, yes,' I placated him. 'There's a horde of your fans right there, drooling into the bouquets they're waiting to present when they ask for your autograph. Maybe I should leave, otherwise my presence might cause a scandal.' I kept moving as I spoke: dabbing my mouth with my napkin, picking up my handbag, standing up, and walking out.

Zhong Liang grabbed me and pulled me into his lap. An unseemly sight – fortunately we were in a private booth.

'It's a returning beast,' he said.

My hairs stood on end.

I jumped to my feet, trying to ignore the warmth emanating from his body, and said, 'Quick, catch him, and ask him to take me to see...'

'Our professor?' Still holding my hand, he cocked an eyebrow at me.

'No.' I tried frantically to shake him off, but his grip was like steel. What martial arts had this little bastard been practicing?

'Do you think I'm an idiot?' he snapped, again with this new side to his personality, all grown-up and firm. With a sigh, still holding me tight, he went on, 'I didn't warn you so you'd go chasing after him. Something's not right about this. I'd feel safer if you went home. Be sure to lock the doors and windows, and don't go wandering off. I'll handle things here.

'Of course,' he added with a wicked smile, 'thanks to this little discussion, the beast has had a chance to get away.'

I stared at him, furious. 'You...' I said, then repeated the word twice more, but I had no idea what would come after that.

He looked at me. 'Do you love him?'

Did I love him? A question I'd never considered, until he asked it. How piercing it sounded.

I looked blankly at this young man. I'd always thought he was just a young man, but all along he'd seen through everything, perfectly clearly. Now he took my hand and asked again, 'Do you?'

'I don't know,' I replied. Love? Still? After all that? Forget it.

My heart was a tangle.

He sighed and pulled over a chair. 'Sit.'

I obediently did as I was told.

He let me go, reached under his shirt collar, and pulled off the red string from around his neck. A pendant dangled from it, something like jade but not jade, warm and glistening.

He placed it in my hand. 'This is a family heirloom, a protective amulet. I'd feel safer if you had it. Bad things keep happening to you. Maybe this will bring you good fortune.'

Something prickled in my eyes, and my vision blurred. I shoved it back at him. 'No, I can't take…'

I broke off.

They say the end of the year is hard to get past – no sooner has one wave subsided when the next arrives.

The pendant lay in my hand, emitting a faint yellow glow. A tiny, unprepossessing thing – no one else would have paid it any attention, but I recognised it. This was one of my professor's most treasured possessions, a relic from an ancient god-beast. I'd seen its data file in the lab, and had asked him if I could have it – it was so pretty. He'd laughed at me. 'It may be pretty, but there's only one of these in the world.'

'So what if there's only one?' I pouted.

'I've already given it to someone,' he had to confess.

'Who?'

'Someone very important to me.' With that, he turned and walked away, which meant the subject was closed forever.

I'd thought of this moment just a few days ago, on my way to the lab. The years slipped away. I could still see his retreating back, and the treasure he must surely have given my mother – who could be more important to him than her?

Instead, unexpectedly, he'd given it to Zhong Liang! Before I'd even met him. Why?

I only hesitated a moment before wrapping my fingers around the fragment of beast bone, clutching it tight so it bit into the tenderness of my palm. 'Thank you,' I said to Zhong Liang.

Thank you. The man before me was looking at me, I was certain, the way my professor must have looked at my mother all those years ago, when he was as young as Zhong Liang now. She was such a beautiful woman, with soft, clear eyes. He must have fallen in love with her right away.

But they hadn't ended up together. In fact, neither of them ever mentioned the other. Why? No living person knew the answer to that.

Zhong Liang smiled at me and tweaked my nose. 'Do as you're told and put this on. I'd feel better if you did. It's very auspicious.'

I felt an enormous pain in my heart, as if it were being drilled into. He walked me to my building. When I said I'd go upstairs on my own, he hesitated a moment before acquiescing. 'Have a good sleep, and I'll take you out tomorrow. I know someone running a toy fair. Plenty of stuffed animals. We could go have a look, and I'll buy you anything that catches your eye. How about that?'

I tamped down the wild beating of my heart and smiled. 'Fine.'

He smiled too, and reached out as if he wanted to stroke my cheek, but didn't. As he left, he said, 'Bye! I hope you won't miss me too much.' Then he spun round, striking a Schwarzenegger pose, and growled, 'I'll be back.' I could have strangled him. The security guard was staring at us.

Seeing my nauseated face, he left satisfied.

I forgot to call the lift, and just stood there, watching his back recede. There was an unfamiliar melancholy about him. He was tall and skinny, with very short hair, both hands in his pockets. No wonder I'd absent-mindedly mistaken him for my professor.

Again, the devil made me open my mouth and call his name. My voice was very soft, so of course, he didn't hear me. Just as well.

I turned and went upstairs. The fragment of beast bone around my neck, which had been icy-cold, gradually warmed up. I still wasn't used to wearing it, and it jabbed against my skin from time to time. In the lift, I looked at my face, now strange to me, existing only for the sake of my mother. As far as he was concerned, the face of a girl he'd once loved.

Not my face.

This wasn't my face.

Once again, I burst into loud sobs.

I couldn't get to sleep that night, turning the bone over in my fingers as my brain buzzed. My professor hadn't changed one bit, I thought – even now that he was dead, he'd still left me plenty of riddles to ensure I wouldn't have a quiet life.

I searched online for information about beast relics, and found nothing. So this really was the only one in the world, and probably no one knew about it except him.

I compared the bone fragment with what I remembered of the diagram in the lab, and it matched perfectly. This was definitely it, but why Zhong Liang? My professor had refused to give it to me, but here it was in my hand anyway. I laughed.

I tossed and turned till half past one, then finally I slept. With the bone dangling over my chest, it felt like returning to the past, and I managed a night without dreams.

When I opened my eyes, I didn't know where I was. Three seconds later, I was groping for my phone, cursing Zhong Liang for phoning me first thing in the morning. Did he want to die?

Even as I muttered the words, I couldn't help smiling.

The shrill beeping of the phone reminded me of the way my professor used to call me a moron, each time my results were off by so much as 0.001. Like an electronic scanner, his eyes saw all. 'Pig-brain,' he would growl. 'Did you take IQ-reducing pills?'

Each time he yelled at me, his eyes bulged and his voice thickened. The windswept genius, the finest of his generation? All that crumbled in an instant. Later on, I learned to make deliberate mistakes to bait him into screaming at me, to entertain me as I sipped my tea and enjoyed an afternoon snack. When he was done, I'd offer him a cup of tea.

I laughed again, and thought I really should tell Zhong Liang about this, and ask if he'd been similarly tortured, oh, and by the way, I was going to make a big stuffed toy in his image, if that was okay with him. That's what was in my head as I grabbed my phone and snapped, 'Why so early?'

But it wasn't Zhong Liang.

Mr Zhong Kui, whose mighty name caused tremors on both sides of the law, was giving me a morning call. 'Is Zhong Liang with you?' he asked.

'No, he's not here.'

'What time did he leave yesterday?'

'Night.' I was still bleary.

'What time?' A rare display of patience from

Zhong Kui.

'About ten.'

'Right, thank you, sorry to disturb you.' He ended the call without waiting for a response.

I sat holding my phone, still not completely awake. It took thirty seconds for the implication to set in. I screamed, covered my mouth, and with shaking hands, phoned Zhong Liang's home. Engaged. Again. Engaged. Again. Still engaged. I tried his mobile. It was off, naturally.

I couldn't be still. I dropped my phone, shivering, and stood up. My head swam. I sat back down, took a deep breath, and stood again. Within five minutes, I'd brushed my teeth and dressed, and was rushing for the lift.

'You're up early, miss,' said Fei the security guard, but I was already out the door.

I got a taxi to Zhong Liang's place. The driver saw the urgency in my face and sped all the way there. I jumped out and rang the doorbell.

Mrs Zhong answered, her usually elegant features for once uncomposed. I clutched at her. 'Zhong Liang...'

Her face was grey. 'He's missing,' she said slowly.

My dear, precious boy.

Zhong Kui was out. Mrs Zhong and I sat alone

in the cavernous living room. The phone was off the hook. 'They'll call my private line if anything comes up,' she explained.

Zhong Liang was missing.

Zhong Kui, who went everywhere and knew everything, said so.

That meant he really was gone. Without needing to ask, I knew that as I'd slept in ignorance, they'd combed every inch of Yong'an, deploying resources and manpower beyond my imagining. And yet, Zhong Liang was missing.

This was no ordinary disappearance. The Zhong family controlled everything, down to the weather itself. It was unthinkable that anyone could be hidden from them in such a tiny city as Yong'an.

I waited with Mrs Zhong in her mansion. She glanced at me from time to time, a hundred emotions in her eyes, changeable as clouds in the wind. First Zhong Ren, and now Zhong Liang. If she'd lunged and sank her teeth into me, I wouldn't have been surprised. But she was Mrs Zhong, and so she sat sedately, and asked the maid to serve me tea. 'Zhong Liang often spoke of you,' she said.

'Oh.'

'He seemed to like you a lot. Were you seeing each other?'

'I don't know.'

I didn't know. My mind was blank. Even my professor's death hadn't left me this bereft. He was dead, that was settled. His corpse was falling apart in its posh tomb. I hadn't visited. He was dead. I was so far away from him, and I didn't know how to get back. There was no way back for us. He was dead.

But Zhong Liang... Zhong Liang...

I stared into space, and tears ran down my cheeks.

Mrs Zhong's eyes reddened in sympathy. 'Don't cry,' she murmured. 'It's a shame your professor is gone, otherwise Zhong Liang would have been fine.'

My professor... An explosion in my head. I fished out the pendant and asked her, 'Does it have anything to do with this?'

She looked, terror blossomed in her eyes, and she shrank into herself.

Slumping back onto the sofa, she wept. 'He gave it to you. He actually gave it to you. I told him never to take it off, and he...'

Her eyes shut, and her voice changed. Hoarse and fluttering, she said, 'Go. No point staying here. Zhong Liang isn't coming back. My son...'

The living room was dark and narrow. The lone lamp cast elongated shadows on the French windows. Suddenly an old woman, Mrs Zhong said, 'He won't be back.'

'Why?' A thousand needles were prickling my heart, and still I had to ask.

'Why...' She took a deep breath and her eyelids sprang open. Her eyes were large and bright, and she was staring straight at me. 'I don't know why. When your professor brought him to us, he said that pendant could never leave the boy's neck, otherwise he'd be taken from us, never to return.'

She was talking to herself. She started struggling to her feet, then huddled into the cushions instead, and stared at the floor. 'He was such a beautiful child, you know. I adored him the moment I set eyes on him. So clever, so handsome...'

I was stone. I didn't hear anything else she said. My professor, now dead, looked down on us like Buddha, eyes half-shut as he regarded the suffering and joy of the mortal world. No matter how far we roamed, we remained in the palm of his hand. His vast shadow pressed down on me. I couldn't breathe. From very far away, I heard the door open, and saw a man walk up to Mrs Zhong. They spoke in low voices. Then he came over and stood in front of me.

I looked up. Zhong Kui.

I didn't even say hello. 'Is Zhong Liang...'

'He's not coming back,' said Zhong Kui. 'He

gave you his pendant.' His eyes were in shadow, and I couldn't make out his expression. 'You should leave,' he said.

'Your wife just said...'

'She said nothing at all.' Zhong Kui's voice was perfectly level. 'You should leave.' He turned and helped Mrs Zhong to her feet. They moved towards the door.

'Wait!' I called after them. 'Just tell me one thing. Is Zhong Liang the professor's son?'

They hesitated a moment. Zhong Kui tried to keep walking, but his wife turned and said, 'No, Zhong Liang was an orphan.'

She stared penetratingly at me, and walked away. Zhong Kui gently stroked her shoulder. She looked so very small.

—

I walked without noticing my surroundings until suddenly it was dark. The streets felt eerily festive. Finally, I got to the Dolphin Bar, where the bartender was watching TV like nothing had happened. My story was my story alone. I sighed, drank, and stroked my pendant. 'Why did he give it to you?' Mrs Zhong had said.

Why? I wanted to know too. *Why, Zhong Liang?*

The answer might be very simple, but who understood him, and who understood my professor? There were wheels within wheels, and I was too clumsy to separate them all.

I remembered the first time I saw Zhong Liang, when my professor sent him with that note for me. He wore a checked shirt, and told me he'd read my stories. My first thought was: so, my professor had a new lapdog.

I'd thought he was just a passer-by in my story, but then he showed up again, and again. Were all my juniors doomed?

I didn't know what was true. My ingenious professor with his theories about everything. *You gave Zhong Liang the pendant. You sent him to me. Why?*

And Zhong Liang – you gave me the pendant. Why?

Out of loyalty, having thought through the risks? Or out of love, having thought through nothing?

Do you love me? No one has ever loved me. The man I thought loved me never did, it was never me at all. I've lived an illusory life. I don't know where I came from, and I don't know where I'll go. Do you know? Do you love me?

I'm so scared, truly scared. In all the vastness of the city, I don't have a single blood relation, no family at all. The woman I thought my mother wasn't actually, and the man I thought I might love was not who I thought he was either.

They lied to me. I'm frightened by how easily I trusted you, how I believed you were someone who loved me. I believed everything.

We are strangers to each other. You don't know my story, and I don't know yours. We poured our hearts into our own stories, but never shared them with each other.

I couldn't stop thinking of Mrs Zhong's final regard. I couldn't read her face, but there was despair in it when she said, 'Zhong Liang was an orphan.'

Whose son are you? Where did you come from? Zhong Liang, with your grinning boyish face, your dry humour, my incorrigible Zhong Liang. If you come back, if you sit before me, quietly take my hand, and tell me everything, I'll love you. I will love you. Never mind if I can't love you, or I already do.

But they said you wouldn't come back. Like a promise, they said you'd been taken, because you gave away your pendant.

Who took you?

I drank my beer, bitter and sharp-tasting. This made no sense. The events of the day before unspooled like a movie. The shocking encounter with the returning beast. The murder. The vomit. The returning beast!

Just like that, I was wide awake. The bar was deathly silent, and all the commotion was outside. What day was it? Without taking his eyes off the TV, the bartender slid another bottle of beer to me. 'Is it New Year's Eve?' I asked.

He looked me in the eye. 'Yes.' A pause. 'Aren't you usually here with that guy?'

'Which one?' I downed my drink and smiled.

He smiled back and gave me a thumbs up. Was this a compliment? We both knew the answer to that.

—

And then it was the new year. The streets exploded with fireworks – the higher-ups had finally lifted the ban. The firework merchants let out the breath they'd held for several years, and started cranking out fire-crackers like little bombs. Everyone was off work, roaming around in bizarre outfits, laughing and sing-ing, beasts and humans alike. Yong'an was a colourful city, really just a giant dance floor. If you dared to completely cut loose, you'd be the darling of the gods.

We were all beloved, celebrating through the night, staying out till we were shit-faced.

At their extremes, pleasure and suffering look the same. I looked at the hysterical faces around me, but Zhong Liang's wasn't among them.

My professor's words abruptly came to me: 'Not one of them is innocent.'

As each firework went off, I stood gaping in

the street. What unspeakable beauty, lasting just an instant. Such exquisite work, brighter than the sun and moon, swaggering into view then vanishing – no evidence it had ever been there, as if it were no more than an illusion.

So many people in the city, so many beasts, and not one of them knew me. The newspapers were all shut for the day, and even my overfamiliar editor was anywhere to be found. Not one phone call. I was starting to miss him.

I called Zhong Liang's house every day and asked if he'd been found. It was always the maid who answered, and each time she told me that he hadn't.

At night, I sat by the entrance to the underpass, waiting for the returning beast to appear from underground so I could grab him and ask, 'Have you seen Zhong Liang? Did you take him?'

He wouldn't dare not confess – I'd inflict on him the worst torments of the Qing Dynasty, till death if necessary. I feared nothing. Had they taken Zhong Liang? If so, was the returning beast who got murdered actually trying to help him?

Knots everywhere I turned, and no one to untie them.

Now I understood how my professor felt. Caring about nothing, black or white alike. I'd lost everything, and only now did I realise I never had anything to start with. What was there to be scared of?

I laughed. If he were still here, I'd call him and he'd answer all my questions. And perhaps he'd add, 'These are basic facts, you moron, how could you not know?'

If only.

I laughed, dazed. Finally, I stood up and raised my arm to stop a taxi. I was going to Yong'an University.

I understood my professor. If there was an afterlife, if he had a soul, he'd tell me. If I went to his lab, I'd know everything. Just like every previous visit. This I believed firmly.

I trusted him.

—

The lab was completely deserted. Through the window, the eucalyptus tree cast its vast shadow. I stood there and just for a moment, it was like returning to the past. Those busy, unknowing, happy days, which would never come again.

I opened his cupboard – the lock was as squeaky as ever – and found his files covered in a thick layer of dust. I unbundled them all and lay them on the ground. Page by page, I searched and searched.

I had no idea what I was looking for, but I knew

my professor would have an answer for me. I kept searching, cursing all the while. 'Stubborn old man. Kept refusing to digitise these – you just used your computer for games. Ridiculous.'

Then a folder with two words that burned into my eyes like a flame: returning beasts.

I opened it. The first item was a sketch – a human woman, very beautiful and perfectly rendered. Clearly my professor's handiwork. She was looking straight at me, her lips slightly parted, as if she had a thousand words to say. Even more arresting was the pregnant swell of her belly.

Before I could think more deeply about it, I'd turned the page and here was the same three-dimensional drawing from our textbook: a scrawny returning beast, hideous face and stark pale skin, red eyes glaring. I'd seen this image hundreds of times while revising for my exams.

Next page. The beast bone pendant, the same picture I'd seen all those years ago, but with some words scrawled underneath. My professor's writing was awful, and I might well have been the only person on earth who could decipher it. 'An artefact with a beastly stench, humans seek but could never possess it.' He must have failed every writing class he'd ever taken – couldn't even explain things simply. I stared at this line, puzzled. What could he mean by this?

The pregnant woman on the first page – could she be Zhong Liang's mother? How was Zhong Liang connected to the returning beasts? And the woman?

Three pictures, laid out like the final question on an exam paper designed to massacre students' brain cells.

I turned the page but the rest of the folder was rubbish, just random things like old exam papers. What a hoarder.

I was still alone, a lost lamb with no one to help me. It hit me again and again that my professor was dead, and I was left with just these desiccated scraps of paper to remember him by. A soul? What nonsense.

He was dead. The dashing scholar, the brightest of his generation, gone, no more.

—

All the way home I had a splitting headache. My brain felt like an obsolete computer, churning away, unable to make sense of the data. All I could hear was Zhong Liang's voice faintly calling me, battering relentlessly at my mind.

If he were here, I would swing around and slap him. The little devil.

The lobby was empty. I stood there a moment,

remembering Zhong Liang standing right there not long ago, posing like Schwarzenegger. My eyes dampened. At that moment, Fei the security guard came by and gave me a strange look. 'Zhong Liang's just gone up,' he said, 'And...'

Zhong Liang!

I flew out of the lift and banged on my door. Zhong Liang opened it – naughty boy, when did he get a copy of my key? – such a handsome young man, his smile like the sun as he said my name.

I thought for a moment this was another hallucination, and held back before throwing my arms around him. 'You bastard! Where the hell were you? How dare you show your face again?'

He hugged me back, and buried his face in my neck. 'Underground,' he answered.

This wasn't real. If I woke up at that moment, I wouldn't have been surprised.

But Zhong Liang really had returned. He pulled me inside, shut the door, and led me to the sofa, where someone was laid out. 'This is my mother.'

A female returning beast.

She was badly hurt, and her breath was ragged. She was grimacing in pain, but when she saw me, she managed a smile.

'Is this...' I was thoroughly confused.

Zhong Liang pulled over a chair for me, and knelt at my feet as if we were in nursery school and I was his teacher. 'My mother,' he said again, gently.

'But she's...'

'She's human,' said Zhong Liang. 'Or at least, she used to be. If she hadn't helped me escape, I would eventually have looked like that too.'

I stared at Zhong Liang, open-mouthed, until I realised how stupid I must appear.

The beast groaned, and Zhong Liang swiftly leaned over to stroke her forehead. 'It's all right,' he murmured, 'It's all right.' The look on his face made my eyes wet again.

'What's wrong?' I finally asked, my voice choked.

'She's dying,' he said calmly.

'Why don't you take her to the hospital...' I cut myself off. I knew why.

The beast looked at me, then at Zhong Liang, and smiled as if she were thinking of the past. 'Don't worry,' she said, 'This will be over soon, and I'll see your father again.'

We said nothing. Zhong Liang was crying too.

The beast beckoned me and took my hand. 'I know how it hurts to lose someone you love,' she said. 'That's why I brought him back to you. When I saw you that night, I knew you were good. You smell different from all the other beasts. No wonder he loves y—'

'Enough,' Zhong Liang interrupted. He took her other hand, avoiding my gaze.

The beast had shut her eyes, but now they sprang open, bulging. 'The bone,' she said, her voice fearful. 'The beast bone...'

I came to my senses and pulled it off my neck. Zhong Liang took it from me, gave me a long look, and put it on.

The beast let out her breath. 'Good,' she said to Zhong Liang. 'They won't find you again. That's good... They're too clever, too complicated, too silent, too tired. You mustn't go back. Take care of yourself, I won't be able to protect you after this.'

She glanced at me, smiled, and raised her hand as if she had something to say. A ghastly rattle came from her throat. Her hand closed tightly around mine, then slackened.

She was dead.

Zhong Liang didn't seem to realise. He remained kneeling by the sofa for a very long time, before turning to me. 'Sit,' he said. 'You must be tired.'

I couldn't speak.

This was Zhong Liang's past, and he hadn't breathed a word about it. I understood now that his innocence didn't come from not knowing anything, but rather from having seen everything there was to see, understanding it, and setting it down. He'd let go of what I hadn't been able to. I knew that now. My professor must have too.

We buried the beast, and Zhong Kui got his beloved son back. Overjoyed, the family did as they were asked, and gave the beast a glorious send-off.

—

We were all at the funeral. Zhong Liang was as handsome as a film star in his black suit, one hand on Mrs Zhong's shoulder, the other in mine. As the gravediggers lowered the coffin, I whispered, 'She's back in the world of spirits now.'

Zhong Liang laughed. 'There's no world of spirits. The people down below—'

'People?'

'Yes.' He turned to me, smiling like this was nothing, thoroughly charming. Bending to my ear, as if this were a private joke, he said, 'All of us here, we're beasts—'

A blaze of light. I knew everything now.

That's what my professor was trying to tell me. 'Not one of us is innocent.'

He'd known all along. When he rescued the

woman from underground, helped her have her baby, and sent the child to live with the Zhong family, he'd known the answer to the riddle. Every one of us had beast blood, pure or half or a quarter or one part in ten thousand. We reeked of beast stench. There was only one piece of beast bone in our world, and in giving it to her son so he could remain undetected, the mother allowed herself to be captured and dragged back to the underworld, My professor kept the child hidden, and eventually brought him to my side. This man who ought to have grown up underground, and me, the beast who'd come out of nowhere. In the vastness of Yong'an, the two of us lived an illusory existence.

I smiled and took Zhong Liang's hand. In the distance, below the hilltop graveyard, the city was slowly being swallowed by the setting sun, all of it glittering in the radiance, so mighty yet so weak, its skyscrapers reduced to shadows. Here's where we came and went, lived and died, our beastly stories playing out here.

What for?

Returning beasts and humans all had their own riddles. Birth as a process of returning, death as a process of longing. To them, this was the most terrifying curse, a catastrophe. Their punishment after their headlong flight.

But to us – ignorant, foolish us – this was nothing at all, just a tender promise between lovers.

—

Returning beasts are not beasts at all, but human. The beasts live in the above-ground city. The stench of the beasts and the filth of the city drove away the humans. They came upon a huge underground cavern, and built a city there. Now there are only beasts left on earth, some pure-blooded, others mixed, going about their business peacefully.

Underground, humans live with no material worries, and a hierarchy of their own. From time to time, though, there is an escape; but these fugitives are always caught, without a single exception. As punishment, they then have to live in caves, where they are whipped, and forced to exist on salt and water, torments too numerous to count. After several years, they become returning beasts.

The returning beasts are sent in pursuit of those who escape, scouring the earth for them. They never fail. Hence their name, for they force the return of all who would flee.

Over thousands of years, the beasts grew foolish and now do not know they are beasts, nor do they recognise humans as people. In this city they built, they have offspring, accept their destinies, fight and make peace, love and hate, grow old and die.

Humans possess intellect, and claim the knowledge of the ages. They take neither sorrow nor joy from material gain or personal loss. Thus their existence is more difficult than necessary, as they strive too hard for cleverness, and push away from the heart. The fugitives fear capture, and the captured fear escape. They live out their days in uncertainty.

What good fortune for the beasts, to lack intelligence; how cursed humans are, that they possess it.

EPILOGUE

It was not yet March when I wrote this book, but spring was already making its presence known. When I was little, I remember older people talking about the willow trees along the river looking green in early spring, and I think this must have been the time of year they were talking about.

This city doesn't have willow trees, so instead, the higher-ups imported little banyan trees from the southernmost tip of the country, their lush aerial roots tangled around their own trunks, evergreen. Come the winter, their crowns had to be shrouded in huge plastic bags that would swell like hot-air balloons with each gust of wind, lifting the entire city into mid-air.

I seldom go out when I'm writing. The farthest I venture is to the supermarket downstairs for snacks – as soon as a story starts, I feel hunger, a gnawing and ravenous hunger.

Suffering through night after night, I shut the

curtains and resisted looking at the outside world. Towards the end, I lay in bed as stiff as steel, aching all over. Finally, I was no longer young.

At long last, I called my editor and said, 'I'm done. Three hundred generations of vengeance, distilled into the torments we inflict upon each other in this life. Now we can turn out the lights and go.'

My editor laughed. 'Enough of that, just send me the manuscript.' I faxed it to him, page after page, reading as I went: unsmiling sorrowful beasts, immortal joyous beasts, martyred sacrificial beasts, unreturning impasse beasts, reincarnated flourishing beasts... Chapter after chapter, all based on my experiences, but when I looked at them again, it all felt so unrealistic, I wondered if any of this had actually happened.

In Yong'an, this familiar yet strange city, beasts hid their true natures as they walked calmly right past you.

I never encountered any of the beasts I wrote about again. The sorrowful beasts' cotton mill went bankrupt, High School 72 was shut down three months ago, and the Temple of the Antiquities was finally torn down during the last round of building works in the city centre, becoming yet another gleaming glass and aluminium shopping complex. As for the prime beasts, after the murder case came to light, a nervous government shut them all up in jail again.

All their legends had come to an end, and no one was looking for new legends.

'You're pure bad luck,' my editor teased.

Whether by coincidence or the murky workings of fate, all my beasts had vanished, leaving behind the stories they'd given me, withered and dry, staring at me.

But stories are stories. Cause and effect are one. Those who write stories are doomed to be toyed with.

The first chapter in this book was squeezed out of me by my editor, whom I must have hurt in a past life. He called me three times in one day, alternately threatening and cajoling. I had a mountain of bills, and no choice but to write. I churned out a tale of sorrowful beasts I'd heard just a few days ago, and shortly after that, as if in a natural progression, the story of the joyous beasts came knocking on my door. One after another, these enormous dark shadows came chasing after me. I wanted to stop, but kept moving ahead, a mere observer to start with, then tumbling into their midst. By the end, when the returning beasts had gone, I'd written what I wanted to write, and I understood my own story. Our sorrows and joys are all our own. A poem instead of tears.

The same clouded blood flows through our veins.

All we have are stories.

The afternoon I finished my manuscript, I took advantage of this rare moment of relaxation to turn on the TV news. A vicious dog attack, a corrupt shopkeeper swindling customers. Strangely, whether today or yesterday, the same few incidents had been broadcast repeatedly. I smiled to myself. I had a long break ahead, and even these stale news items would be fascinating.

Then, right at the end, something different for once: an explosion of unrest at an asylum in the suburbs, during which countless patients had escaped. The police were doing their best to catch them all, and in the meantime, residents were urged to take precautions.

The camera panned across the chaos of the institution. A doctor in his white coat, looking as hapless as one of his patients, said, 'I don't know how it happened, they just ran...' He would have sobbed, but he had no tears left.

He was cute, like my former therapist. Something vindictive reared its head in me, and I burst out laughing.

This was joyful. I felt carefree.

Before I was done laughing, the phone rang. I picked up, and an unfamiliar male voice said my name. 'I'll be waiting for you at the Dolphin Bar.'

'Who are you?' I said, startled.

'Charley.'

'Charley!' Even more startling. Charley who'd been locked up in an asylum, Charley who'd been a sacrificial beast – and sacrificial beasts had once been gods.

—

There was Charley at the Dolphin Bar, the same mischievous grin on his face.

I sat across from him, and because I didn't know what to talk about, all I said was, 'Charley.'

He smiled frankly. 'Good to see you. I know what you've been going through.'

'How would you know?'

'Your weekly series in the city paper.'

So that was it. Countless people read my stories each week in the newspaper, and they'd write me letters to commiserate, or to praise me, or to yell at me for making it all up – but god knows every word I wrote was the bloody truth, my own regret and pain. I must be the most foolish author in the world, slicing my heart open and displaying it to strangers, but none of you know – no one does – that all my beasts have vanished, and now no one believes they were real, and no one even understands why I laid them out for you. I don't understand it myself.

Apart from those in the stories, that is. Apart from Charley.

He said, 'I came to say goodbye. Your book is done, and the story of the sacrificial beasts was finished long ago. I ought to leave this place.'

'Why?'

'People should leave when their story is over,' he said. 'Don't you know that?'

'Does that mean the other beasts will carry on?'

'I know there's a knot in your heart still. I'm here to untie it for you.'

'What is it?' I was puzzled.

'They both loved you very much,' said Charley. I sat staring at him. He'd answered the question I'd asked myself a thousand times, without ever being able to speak the words. Tears came to my eyes.

'Don't cry,' said Charley, smiling. 'Your mother was a beast too, a bloodletting beast. They adored each other, but couldn't be together, nor could they have offspring. And so, together, they created you. Do you know why they called you the heartsick beast?'

And in that instant, I did know. My professor putting his arms around me and saying, 'This is my heartsick beast. My heart is sick for you.'

I shut my eyes and smiled.

My father and mother. How did they fall in love? Why couldn't they stay together? I didn't know, but that didn't matter. They loved each other, and they loved me. That was enough.

'How do you know?' I opened my eyes and looked at him.

'That's a secret.'

This vast city, the beasts that come and go, all of this, is a secret. No one knows why they come or why they go, why they meet or why they leave. These are all enormous, distant mysteries.

Our grubby, foolish souls worship this vastness, and in the end, we are grateful.

I walked Charley to the door of the Dolphin Bar. Just like so many times before, he waved and said, 'See you later.'

I waved too, and said I'd see him later.

We went our separate ways, and were soon swallowed whole by the tangled streets of the city, even if that meant we would never see each other again.

—

Zhong Liang showed up that evening to take me to dinner, a celebration for finishing my book. He helped himself to an apple and said, 'If we got married, would you want pink roses or lilies?'

I raised my eyebrows. 'Could this be a proposal?'

He smiled bashfully.

I smiled too. 'How about gardenias? They're commonplace, but lovely, and just a little fragrant.'

Spring would pass into summer, and soon the streets would be full of old women selling gardenias, fifty cents a bunch, so cheap and abundant.

In the summer, everyone in Yong'an would be able to read this book. People and beasts would read these stories and say, 'Where did she get these ideas from?' That's how forgetful an industrial city is.

It doesn't matter. I wrote them to amuse you. Go ahead and smile at all my love and hatred. It's just weather. That's okay.

Or perhaps no one will understand which city I'm talking about. I called it Yong'an for eternal peace, a blessing of sorts. That's how authors are; the words we write are fleeting, but what goes unsaid is eternal as rock.

There is a city in the south that is full of beasts – beasts who rage and love, gather and leave, just as humans do.

This book has been selected to receive financial assistance from English PEN's "PEN Translates" programme, supported by Arts Council England. English PEN exists to promote literature and our understanding of it, to uphold writers' freedoms around the world, to campaign against the persecution and imprisonment of writers for stating their views, and to promote the friendly co-operation of writers and the free exchange of ideas. www.englishpen.org

tiltedaxispress.com

ISBN (paperback)   9781911284444
ISBN (ebook)   9781911284437

A catalogue record for this book is available from the British Library.

Edited by Saba Ahmed
Cover design by Soraya Gilanni Viljoen
Typesetting and ebook production by Simon Collinson
Printed and bound by Clays Ltd, Elcograf S.p.A.

Supported using public funding by
ARTS COUNCIL ENGLAND

ENGLISH PEN

ABOUT TILTED AXIS PRESS

Tilted Axis is a non-profit press publishing mainly work by Asian writers, translated into a variety of Englishes. This is an artistic project, for the benefit of readers who would not otherwise have access to the work – including ourselves. We publish what we find personally compelling.

Founded in 2015, we are based in the UK, a state whose former and current imperialism severely impacts writers in the majority world. This position, and those of our individual members, informs our practice, which is also an ongoing exploration into alternatives – to the hierarchisation of certain languages and forms, including forms of translation; to the monoculture of globalisation; to cultural, narrative, and visual stereotypes; to the commercialisation and celebrification of literature and literary translation.

We value the work of translation and translators through fair, transparent pay, public acknowledgement, and respectful communication. We are dedicated to improving access to the industry, through translator mentorships, paid publishing internships, open calls and guest curation.

Our publishing is a work in progress – we are always open to feedback, including constructive criticism, and suggestions for collaborations. We are particularly keen to connect with Black and indigenous translators of Asian languages.

tiltedaxispress.com

@TiltedAxisPress